## RAND

# New Challenges for International Leadership

## Lessons from Organizations with Global Missions

Tora K. Bikson, Gregory F. Treverton, Joy Moini, Gustav Lindstrom

Supported by the
Starr Foundation, the Rockefeller Brothers Fund,
the United Nations Foundation, and RAND

**National Security Research Division**

The research described in this report was sponsored chiefly by a grant from the Starr Foundation, with supplemental funding from the Rockefeller Brothers Fund, the United Nations Foundation, and RAND. The research was conducted through the International Programs and Development unit of RAND's National Security Research Division (NSRD).

**Library of Congress Cataloging-in-Publication Data**

New challenges for international leadership : lessons from organizations with global missions / Tora K. Bikson, Gregory F. Treverton, Joy Moini, Gustav Lindstrom.
    p. cm.
    "MR-1670."
    ISBN 0-8330-3345-X (pbk.)
    1. Leadership. 2. International business enterprises—Management. 3. Organizational effectiveness.  I. Bikson, Tora K., 1940–

HD57.7.N488 2003
658.4'092—dc21

                                 2003002675

RAND is a nonprofit institution that helps improve policy and decisionmaking through research and analysis. RAND® is a registered trademark. RAND's publications do not necessarily reflect the opinions or policies of its research sponsors.

Published 2003 by RAND
1700 Main Street, P.O. Box 2138, Santa Monica, CA 90407-2138
1200 South Hayes Street, Arlington, VA 22202-5050
201 North Craig Street, Suite 202, Pittsburgh, PA 15213-1516
RAND URL: http://www.rand.org/
To order RAND documents or to obtain additional information, contact Distribution Services: Telephone: (310) 451-7002; Fax: (310) 451-6915; Email: order@rand.org

**PREFACE**

Is the United States producing the leaders it will need in the 21st century? The research reported here (*New Challenges for International Leadership: Lessons from Organizations with Global Missions*, MR-1670-IP) was undertaken to address this question. It was prompted by concerns about America's capacity to develop among its people the intellectual and professional expertise that will be required for leadership in the increasingly globalized environment of the 21st century.

RAND proposed to explore this issue by interviewing representatives of internationally oriented organizations, which confront these questions daily, as well as by querying experts who could provide insights into the answers to those questions (see Appendixes A and B). We also proposed to review recent literature on this topic. The results of that effort are available in a separate RAND report by Gustav Lindstrom, Tora K. Bikson, and Gregory F. Treverton (*Developing America's Leaders for a Globalized Environment: Lessons from Literature Across Public and Private Sectors*, MR-1627-IP, 2002). Themes emerging from these research activities are further explored in Issue Papers by Gregory F. Treverton and Tora K. Bikson (*New Challenges for International Leadership: Positioning the United States for the 21st Century*, IP-233-IP, 2002) and by Paul Light (*Rebuilding The Supply Chain of Foreign Affairs Leaders*, IP-244-IP, 2002).

The project was supported chiefly by a grant from the Starr Foundation, with supplemental funding from the Rockefeller Brothers Fund, the United Nations Foundation, and RAND. It was guided by an advisory council made up of the leaders of major foreign affairs institutions—the Council on Foreign Relations, American Enterprise Institute, American International Group, Inc., The Brookings Institution, Carnegie Endowment for International Peace, Center for

Strategic and International Studies, The Heritage Foundation, The Nixon Center, and the US Institute of Peace, as well as RAND.

The work reflected in this report draws on and contributes to a body of RAND research on workforce planning and professional development. It also contributes to a growing body of RAND research on emerging human resource needs as they are affected by changing organizational requirements in general and the pressures of increasing internationalization in particular. The findings should be of interest to US policymakers who aim to enhance America's ability to exercise its global role effectively in the century that lies ahead. They should also be useful to decisionmakers in all organizations whose missions have an international reach, whether in the public, for-profit, or non-profit sectors. Finally, they should inform researchers and practitioners in organizations that aim to improve the fit between internationally oriented human resource needs and the supply of talent available to fulfill them—universities, management consulting and development firms, and recruiting organizations).

The project was housed within RAND's National Security Research Division (NSRD), under the International Programs and Development unit. Directed by Jerrold Green, the program's mission is to take on global policy research questions that cut across functional disciplines and regional boundaries, eclipsing old patterns of state-to-state relations. Complex issues such as international security, transnational trade and investment, education, health care, information technology, and energy and environment are all topics that benefit from the multidisciplinary, uncompromising analytic approach of researchers in NSRD's International Programs.

International Programs is part of RAND's National Security Research Division (NSRD). NSRD conducts research and analysis for a broad range of clients including the US Department of Defense, the intelligence community, allied foreign governments, and foundations.

For more information about international studies at RAND, contact Jerrold Green (+1-310-393-0411, x6903 or Jerrold_Green@rand.org).  For more information about this project, contact Tora Bikson (+1-310-393-0411, x7227 or Tora_Bikson@rand.org).

# CONTENTS

**TABLES**

## SUMMARY

Is the United States producing the leaders it will need in the
21st century?  No issue is more critical for America's role in the world
than its capacity to develop among its people the intellectual and
professional expertise that will be required for leadership in
international affairs.

We confront, today, a world that that bears little resemblance to
that of a few decades ago.  It is both networked and fractured, both
full of promise and full of danger.  Although information and
communication technology now link countries and organizations in
unprecedented ways, cultural, political, and economic differences
constitute significant barriers to international understanding.
Exercising leadership in this environment presents new and daunting
challenges.  The bipolar world view that characterized the cold war
period has given way to a global perspective in which national
boundaries no longer define the limits of daily interaction in
government and business.

The events of September 11, 2001, underscored the importance of
developing a broader and deeper understanding of the differing
perspectives of people from other countries and other cultures and of
learning to work effectively with people who differ in language,
customs, and, in some cases, political and social values.  The global
role of the United States in the century ahead will demand greater
understanding of the economic, political, and cultural forces that shape
the world.  And, while the aftermath of September 11 has given new
urgency to the role of national governments, it has also called
attention to the significant parts played in world affairs by the
private sectors.  International leadership is not for governments alone;
it is exerted as well by corporations, nongovernmental institutions, and
intergovernmental organizations.  Thus the need for a globally competent

workforce spans these sectors, characterizing all organizations with an international reach.

**OBJECTIVES**

Against this background, the study reported here aims to improve public understanding and enrich public discussion of the challenges the United States faces in building the cross-cultural expertise that will be required for international leadership in the 21st century. Toward that end, it addresses the following research questions.

- How have recent trends toward globalization affected major public and private sector organizations in general and their human resource needs in particular?

- What kinds of competencies are now being sought in career professionals in organizations whose missions have an international dimension?

- How, and how well, are these human resource needs being met?

- What are the prospects for meeting future internationally oriented human resource needs?

- What policies and practices are likely to improve the development of capabilities for leadership in public and private sector organizations in the global environment of the 21st century?

In what follows, we first briefly outline the study's research methods and then summarize the chief conclusions and recommendations.

**RESEARCH APPROACH**

The study's research approach is based on work done in two prior RAND projects (Berryman et al., 1979; Bikson and Law, 1994), along with findings from an extensive literature review conducted for this project (Lindstrom, Bikson, and Treverton, 2002). Primary data are drawn from structured interviews with 135 human resource managers and senior managers from 75 organizations divided equally among the public, for-profit and non-profit sectors. Organizations were selected on the basis of two criteria: They had to have international missions that engage them in interactions spanning national boundaries, and they had to have been in existence long enough to have experienced the effects of increasing globalization. (The attained sample is listed in Appendix A.)

Typically the human resources representative was selected first; that individual then identified managers within their organizations who played a significant role in a border-spanning business process. The interviewees were distributed among kinds of organizations and roles within organizations as shown in Table S.1.

**Table S.1 Research Participants by Role and Sector**

| Role | Sector | | | |
|------|--------|--------|--------|--------|
| | Public | For-profit | Non-profit | Total |
| Human resources | 19 | 21 | 26 | 66 |
| Line management | 22 | 21 | 26 | 69 |
| Total | 41 | 42 | 52 | 135 |

Interviews were guided by a written protocol to ensure that comparable information relevant to the key research objectives outlined above would be collected systematically across participants. In the interviews, we explored effects of globalization and probed in some detail the need for new competencies to respond to the requirements of globalization. After identifying needed skills, interviewees were first asked about their views as to how well these needs are being met, and they were then asked to comment on postemployment development and other efforts intended to yield higher-level cadres of internationally capable managers and professionals within their organizations and in society more broadly. Finally, they were asked to describe the issues, problems, and prospects of globalization facing their organizations. Incorporating both close-ended and open-ended items, the protocol was flexible enough to elicit rich and wide-ranging responses.

To complement and extend what we learned from these structured interviews, we discussed the emerging issues of globalization as they relate to private firms, non-profit organizations, and governmental institutions in the United States with 24 individuals selected on the basis of nominations from the project's advisory committee, their established expertise in domains of interest, their contributions to relevant literature, or all of these. (They are acknowledged in Appendix B.)  In a series of unstructured interviews, we undertook to elicit from these individuals their insights into the kinds of policies and practices that could improve the development of leadership capabilities in internationally oriented organizations.

## GLOBAL LEADERSHIP SKILLS: DEMAND AND SUPPLY

Increasing globalization has created an environment that makes the exercise of international leadership significantly more complex.  High-level officers of public, for-profit, and non-profit organizations must interact with one another across borders to arrive at negotiated decisions about issues that often blend advances in science and technology with policy concerns, while blurring the distinctions between foreign and domestic affairs.  Moreover, globalization is not just concerned with economics and finance; it has significant political, legal and sociocultural dimensions—both positive and negative—that have become increasingly salient to organizations with international missions since September 11, 2001.  The public sector got off to a slower start in coping with the broad and complex implications of globalization than the other two sectors, but, since September 11, it has been moving quickly to catch up.  Other sectors globalized faster as corporations sought broader markets and non-profits engaged new partners.

### International Managers Need an Integrated Skill Repertoire

To exercise leadership effectively in this environment, senior managers and professionals need a multidimensional and well-integrated set of competencies.  There are some between-sector differences in how highly particular competencies (e.g., substantive domain knowledge, competitiveness and drive, foreign language fluency versus English language communication skills) are valued, but our interviewees agree that international leaders must have an integrated repertoire of skills including the following:

- *Substantive depth (professional or technical knowledge) related to the organization's primary business processes.*

  Without this depth, leaders cannot make sound decisions about risks and opportunities and will not gain the respect and trust of those below them.

- *Managerial ability, with an emphasis on teamwork and interpersonal skills.*

  This ability is needed not only to work with different partners but also because within organizations a great deal of decisionmaking is being pushed to lower hierarchical levels, so that upper- and lower-level decisions become more collaborative.

- *Strategic international understanding.*

  It is critical for leaders to have a strategic vision of where the organization is going and to place it in a global context while understanding the implications of operating in different localities.

- *Cross-cultural experience.*

  Multicultural sensitivity cannot readily be gained through academic instruction alone. Efforts to learn a second or third language provide evidence of interest in other cultures and can form a basis for understanding them, but are not a substitute for real world experience.

**Demographic Trends Portend Significant Skill Deficits**

This skill repertoire is seen as being in great demand but in short supply, with the result that our interviewees expect major skill deficits in the international leadership cadre in the near future. Today's senior managers and professionals, drawn from the baby boom generation, are nearing retirement; at the same time, the downsizing and streamlining strategies of the 1980s and early 1990s severely reduced the middle management tier. Further, those who remain in the successor cohort do not appear to have the required competencies for leadership in this changed world. While the demographic and cohort dimensions of this problem cross sectors, the anticipated leadership gap is most acute in federal agencies; in describing the future public sector workforce, some have called it a "human capital crisis."

**Career Development Programs Ineffective for Preparing Global Leaders**

Postemployment education and development programs could, in principle, address the competency shortfall described above. But such programs are generally systematically designed and widely offered only at the point of entry for new employees. However, this is where the gaps between needed and available competencies are generally smallest. Regarding entry-level employees, interviewees from the organizations participating in our study are, with some exceptions, fairly well satisfied with the products of US universities. (The exceptions include a dearth of science and technology graduates who are US citizens, of graduates with fluency in uncommon languages, of US minorities majoring in graduate studies relevant to international careers, and of graduates with international experience.) Typically, there is little need or opportunity for entry-level employees to exert leadership skills in an international environment, but these young people are seen as having the potential to do so.

At lower hierarchical levels, there are, however, alternatives to recruiting individuals with the requisite skills or developing these skills in postemployment training programs. These alternatives include contracting out (e.g., in the case of language services), hiring non-US citizens (e.g., in the case of scientists and engineers), and establishing internships and cooperative programs (e.g., for providing desired integrative experiences in real performance settings). There are drawbacks both to outsourcing (e.g., loss of institutional memory) and to hiring of foreign nationals (e.g., visas may become harder to get in the future), but for now both are viable and widely used approaches for coping with some competency shortages. Networked information and communication technologies may also be deployed more effectively in the future to access hard-to-get skills.

The shortage of employees with the desired repertoire of skills is greatest at mid-career levels and beyond. Paradoxically, this is the period when professional education and development offerings become markedly less well defined and—in the for-profit and non-profit sectors—less frequently available as well.  More important, the offerings typically provided are not well suited to yield the desired results.

Most often, career development at higher levels is self-initiated, ad hoc, and unrelated to an organization's strategic plans.  It may involve activities undertaken in order to check off a requirement or to move up a rung on a career ladder at the next performance review; or it may be a reward bestowed on those who have already demonstrated advanced leadership capabilities.  Further, the most frequently used development approaches (e.g., courses) are the least robust, while stronger programs (e.g., job rotation, especially to a non-US site) are much less often employed.  Present patterns of investment in human resource development are thus not likely to produce the needed repertoire of skills within the leadership cadre of international organizations.

## Lateral Hiring Rarely Serves to Reduce Global Leadership Skill Deficits

Lateral hiring from organizations within or outside the sector is the second potential route for remedying competency shortfalls and providing fresh perspectives at mid-career and higher levels in international organizations.  But, as with career development programs, it is not, as presently practiced, likely to produce the mix of leadership competencies these organizations seek.

On the one hand, intramural stovepipes tend to be replicated across organizations.  That is, lateral entrants are very likely to be drawn not only from the same sector but also from very similar, narrowly defined subdomains.  Such an approach assures substantive expertise and avoids the culture shock of cross-sector transitions, but it decreases the chances of innovation and growth both for the organization and the mid-career employee.  On the other hand, cross-sector moves, while holding developmental promise for organizations and their later-career hires, are more risky, and such moves lack institutionalized support structures.

The public sector is at a special disadvantage for cross-sector lateral hiring at upper levels because its salary scale is not competitive and because its rules constrain the exit of its own upper-level people to other sectors.

## MEETING THE DEMAND: PROBLEMS AND PROSPECTS

The end result is that the outlook for future leadership in international organizations is very mixed—there are envisioned problems as well as promising prospects. The bad news is that, at present, these organizations lack the multidimensional competencies in their human resources that future leadership cadres will need to carry out their global missions effectively. The good news is that contemporary demographic and cohort factors combine to create an unprecedented opportunity for organizations with a global reach to repopulate their upper ranks.

Further, participants in this research believe that career candidates today are generally more interested in and knowledgeable about international affairs than prior cohorts. In addition, they are more willing to embrace mobile careers, and a larger proportion now report wanting to contribute to large-scale societal goals. Thus the public sector stands to be affected most severely by the problems that lie ahead, but also stands to benefit greatly from the most promising prospects.

## RECOMMENDATIONS: DEVELOPING LEADERS FOR THE GLOBAL ENVIRONMENT

What, then, can be done to take advantage of the opportunities created by the shifting demographics of the workforce and the skills and interests of these new workers to produce competent international leadership in US organizations? We recommend that US organizations that have an international reach or that are involved in preparing individuals for careers that involve an international component take the following actions.

- Encourage the development of portfolio careers.
- Develop personnel policies to support portfolio careers.
- Internationalize university curricula.
- Implement sector-specific near-term and long-term programs to develop international leaders.

## Encourage the Development of Portfolio Careers

We recommend providing a mix of innovative, robust development approaches for those in mid-career and higher positions and introducing measures to facilitate the kinds of transitions between such posts that, in the end, make for the kinds of career portfolios that all sectors desire for their leaders.

Enabling the pursuit of portfolio careers will require changing mind-sets in all three sectors. The for-profit sector still prefers to grow talent within, while non-profit and public sector officials live their careers in narrow stovepipes. Within the government, the first step is to make it easier for people to move across agencies. In some areas, such as intelligence, it might be possible to mimic the experience of the military Joint Staff, making rotations to other agencies or "joint" appointments a requirement. The existing Intergovernmental Personnel Act (IPA) makes it possible for people to move across agencies but does not make it easy or desirable. The provisions of this act should be expanded, possibly through new legislation, and become a distinguished learning opportunity, as should other programs that detail government officials to the Congress, to state and local governments, or to the private sector.

The for-profit sector should begin to think of the other sectors as partners in developing future leaders. Like government, it draws on the other sectors, particularly government diplomats and military officers, for internationally oriented leaders at the top. It does not, however, think of moving its younger executives into other sectors as a way to broaden their experience.

The not-for-profit sector could play a special role in developing portfolio careers. Foundations like Ford and MacArthur have developed innovative programs for giving young people dual expertise, in area studies as well as strategy, or policy as well as science. Such opportunities could be expanded, with the specific goal of producing future leaders in all sectors with international experience and exposure.

**Develop Personnel Policies and Practices to Support Portfolio Careers**

To support portfolio careers, the policies and strategies of human resource units and the international organizations they serve would have to change. First, human resource units will have to become strategic partners with top-level decisionmakers charged with shaping the organization's future missions. In that capacity, they should look more broadly—even across sectors—for best practices to adopt, adapt, and implement for developing multidimensional competency repertoires in their in-house career professionals and for facilitating cross-sector lateral transitions at mid-career levels and beyond. Further, human resource units should collaborate more closely with line managers in deciding to take more risks with employee assignments (e.g., stretch assignments, especially those that involve overseas work).

Moreover, human resource units should better exploit the flexibilities that exist in current regulations and policies, while formulating new policies better designed to meet today's needs for international expertise at higher levels of organizations. The public sector faces greater challenges in this area because it has special obstacles to overcome (e.g., time-consuming hiring processes, constraints on hiring non-US citizens, and noncompetitive salaries).

**Internationalize University Curricula**

In addition, to improve the supply side, the nation's education institutions need to rethink curricula and practices as they seek to produce more internationally minded leaders. They have found it easier to internationalize their faculties than their curricula, and many non-Americans now teach at America's universities. Most of those, however, have Ph.D.s from the same US universities as their American counterparts. So, these non-American faculty members with US Ph.D.s are the beginning of internationalizing, not the end.

The traditional ways that universities conceived of "internationalizing" their curriculums--by developing academic area studies and language training--may no longer be the best ways of producing broad-gauged professionals. Instead, universities need to devise ways to give students a grounding in thinking and acting across cultures. In particular, they should ask why so many college students arrive saying that they intend to take a year of study abroad but so few actually do so. Experiences abroad shorter than a year or semester, and more oriented toward professional tasks, might be valuable. And, given the explosion of non-Americans and of cultural diversity on many US campuses, innovative approaches could produce cross-cultural competence while remaining at home.

It is striking that internationally oriented organizations in all three sectors stress the need for a new cadre of leaders, and leadership programs are widely available in academic institutions. Yet leadership remains something of an outcast in American higher education. It is not quite academic, hence not quite respectable. Yet if leaders, like entrepreneurs (or scholars) are partly born, leadership skills can also be developed. Producing effective leadership deserves a much more prominent place in the nation's research and teaching.

**Implement Near- and Long-Term International Leadership Development**

The agenda for better positioning tomorrow's America to lead in a globalized world requires actions by all three sectors represented in this study, plus higher education--ideally in partnership. Table S.2 summarizes the chief recommendations from the study, by sector, according to whether they could feasibly be pursued to affect expected near-term international leadership gaps (first column) or would take longer and more complex implementation efforts but would address identified needs to build future cohorts of international managers and professionals. Both courses should be pursued concurrently.

**Table S.2 Recommended Agenda for Building International Leadership**

| | Time Horizon | |
|---|---|---|
| | **Shorter Term--The Current Workforce** | **Longer Term--The Pipeline** |
| **Public** | • Increase and enhance use of IPAs<br>• Facilitate lateral movement inside and outside government<br>• Improve hiring processes<br>• Target robust career development programs | • Expand internship and cooperative programs<br>• Narrowly target fellowships in areas of need<br>• Support and encourage portfolio careers<br>• Relax barriers to in-and-out careers (e.g., conflict of interest laws)<br>• Fund leadership development research<br>• Reserve some proportion of senior positions in any agency for the career service |
| **For-profit** | • Support career exchanges with public and non-profit sectors<br>• Target robust career development programs | • Support and encourage portfolio careers<br>• Support internationalized MBA programs |
| **Non-profit** | • Support career exchanges with public and for-profit sectors<br>• Heighten awareness of need for future leaders<br>• Improve hiring processes<br>• Target robust career development programs | • Increase funding for producing dual (and treble) expertise<br>• Increase support for leadership study and training<br>• Articulate and support study of specialized human resource needs of international non-profit organizations (both nongovernmental and intergovernmental) |
| **Higher Education** | • Promote and recognize real world study abroad<br>• Expand initiatives for internationalizing education at home | • Internationalize graduate programs in relevant areas (e.g., MPA, MPP, MBA, IP, and related doctoral studies)<br>• Rethink ways to internationalize other curricula<br>• Improve US minority recruitment/retention in international programs<br>• Give leadership development a serious place in teaching and research |

Notes: MPA – Master in public administration
MPP – Master in public policy
MBA – Master in business administration
IP – International policy

In the end, it will not be easy to respond to the challenges of 21st century leadership. In part that is because of the complexity of the global environment that today's international organizations face. Another major difficulty is that effective responses to these challenges must be distributed over myriad organizations and will have to be largely self-generated--no one-size-fits-all solutions are in sight.

Organizations—and nations—that address these leadership challenges successfully will have a competitive advantage in the decades to come.

## ACKNOWLEDGMENTS

We are indebted to the organizations represented on the project's advisory board—the Council on Foreign Relations, American Enterprise Institute, American International Group, Inc., The Brookings Institution, Carnegie Endowment for International Peace, Center for Strategic and International Studies, The Heritage Foundation, The Nixon Center, and the US Institute of Peace, as well as RAND—for their help in developing this research. We especially want to recognize the efforts of board members Frank Wisner and Richard Solomon, who, true to the group's purpose, offered thoughtful advice throughout the course of the project.

We would also like to acknowledge a number of colleagues at RAND for their contributions to the project. Special thanks go to research assistant Dionne Barnes for her invaluable help with data collection and to Michael Woodward for setting up and maintaining the project database as well as for his assistance with manuscript preparation. Jolene Galegher provided timely and expert guidance during the editing of the final report. We are particularly grateful to Dean Joseph Nye (Kennedy School of Government) and Paul Light (Senior Fellow, The Brookings Institution) for insightful reviews of an earlier draft; the final report benefited significantly from their comments and suggestions.

Finally, we wish to thank the public, for-profit, nongovernmental, and intergovernmental organizations that took part in the study. Their representatives made time available to cooperate in the research, candidly sharing their knowledge and experience. We learned a great deal from them.

# CHAPTER ONE.  INTRODUCTION

Is the United States producing the leaders it will need in the 21st century?  No issue is more critical for America's role in the world than its capacity to develop among its people the intellectual and professional expertise that will be required for leadership in international affairs, and that issue has never been more important than it is today.

Our world now bears little resemblance to that of a few decades ago.  The bipolar worldview that characterized the cold war period has given way to a global perspective in which national boundaries no longer define the limits of daily interaction in business, government, and nongovernmental organizations.  Advances in information and communication technology have facilitated this process, linking countries and organizations in unprecedented ways, but cultural, political, and economic differences constitute significant barriers to international understanding.  Today's world is both networked and fractured, both full of promise and full of danger.  Exercising leadership in this environment presents new and daunting challenges.

The events of September 11, 2001, underscored the importance of developing a broader and deeper understanding of the differing perspectives of people from other countries and other cultures and of learning to work effectively with people who differ in language, customs, and, in some cases, political and social values.  The global role of the United States in the century ahead will demand greater understanding of the economic, political, and cultural forces that shape the world.  And, while the aftermath of September 11 has given new urgency to the role of national governments, it has also called attention to the significant parts played in world affairs by the private sectors.  International leadership is not for governments alone; it is exerted as well by corporations, nongovernmental institutions, and intergovernmental organizations. Thus the need for a globally competent workforce spans these sectors, characterizing all organizations with an international reach.

Against this background, the study reported here aims to improve public understanding and enrich public discussion of the challenges the United States faces in building the cross-cultural expertise that will be required for international leadership in the 21st century.[1] Toward that end, it addresses the following research questions.

- *How have recent trends toward globalization affected major public and private sector organizations in general and their human resource needs in particular?*

- *What kinds of competencies are now being sought in career professionals in organizations whose missions have an international dimension?*

- *How, and how well, are these human resource needs being met?*

- *What are the prospects for meeting future internationally oriented human resource needs?*

- *What policies and practices are likely to improve the development of capabilities for leadership in public and private sector organizations in the global environment of the 21st century?*

In what follows, we first provide a brief account of the background and conceptual framework for the study. Next we describe the research methods and results. We end with a discussion of conclusions and recommendations.

---

1 The research reported here is part of a larger study funded chiefly by the Starr Foundation, with supplemental support from the Rockefeller Brothers Fund, the United Nations Foundation, and RAND. It was guided by an advisory committee made up of the leaders of major foreign affairs institutions: the Council on Foreign Relations, American Enterprise Institute, American International Group, Inc., The Brookings Institution, Carnegie Endowment for International Peace, Center for Strategic and International Studies, The Heritage Foundation, The Nixon Center, and the US Institute of Peace, as well as RAND.

## CHAPTER TWO.   CONCEPTUAL FRAMEWORK AND BACKGROUND

As a foundation for pursuing these research objectives, we relied heavily on two prior RAND studies examining the supply of and demand for international expertise in public sector institutions (Berryman et al., 1979) and private sector firms (Bikson and Law, 1994) with international missions.  We also undertook an extensive review of more recent literature in this field to take into account the growing significance of globalization and its human resource implications.  The updated review also sought to learn what is known about the human resource needs of internationally oriented nongovernmental and intergovernmental non-profit organizations (see Lindstrom, Bikson, and Treverton, et al. 2002, and the bibliography below).  Here we summarize the main themes emerging from this background work that frame our research approach.

### GLOBALIZATION

It is appropriate to begin with globalization, which is a comparatively recent driver of human resource needs in US organizations. For purposes of this project, we treat globalization as the expansion of networks of interdependence spanning national boundaries that follows the increasingly rapid movement of information, ideas, money, goods, services, and people across those borders (Nye and Keohane, 1987). Globalization in this sense is accelerated by advances in information and communication technologies (Malone and Crowston, 2001).  Although its economic implications received greatest initial attention (Bikson and Law, 1994), its political, legal, and sociocultural dimensions have increased in salience in recent years—and especially so after the events of September 11.

So defined, globalization has several important implications for this study.  First, in previous decades, international leadership was mainly viewed as the province of a small number of federal agencies—the

State Department, the Department of Defense, and the national security agencies.

Presently, however, a great many federal agencies have missions that incorporate significant and far-reaching international dimensions—Agriculture, Environment, Commerce, Health, and Labor, among others. Besides broadening the demand for international competencies in the federal workforce, these changes eventuate in some blurring of the boundaries between domestic and foreign policy.

Second, globalization also entails de facto sharing of international leadership among a broader range of stakeholders. Although national governments continue to play key roles, international leadership is also exercised by multinational corporations as well as by major private nongovernmental and intergovernmental non-profit organizations. As a result, both formal and collegial partnerships that span sectors as well as national borders are increasingly in evidence. The implication is that a study of the challenges to international leadership in the 21st century should take all three sectors into account.

**NEW COMPETENCY NEEDS**

The changes stimulated by globalization should lead, in turn, to changed human resource requirements in the affected organizations. In their study of multinational corporations, for example, Bikson and Law (1994) reported a demand for two generic new characteristics. One is cognitive—a revolutionary way of understanding the structure of the world economy and the position of US firms within it (a "Copernican revolution" in which the US-centric perspective gives way to an astronaut's view of the global business environment). The other is operational, reflecting the skills and attitudes necessary to translate that understanding into new ways of performing business missions that are more responsive to local opportunities and threats. A somewhat similar set of changed human resource requirements might be forthcoming for public sector organizations if, as Nye (2002) sees it, globalism entails the vision of US agencies "embodied in a web of multilateral institutions that allow others to participate in decisions."

The literature review confirms that organizations whose missions have an international component are, indeed, looking for new competencies while not abandoning their traditional requirements for entering career employees (Lindstrom, Bikson, and Treverton, 2002). However, we did not identify a limited and widely agreed upon set of desirable characteristics. Rather, the articles we reviewed yield a sizeable number of partially overlapping lists of attributes; most are organization specific and their importance has not been empirically validated. On the other hand, at the typological level, the literature converges on a threefold categorization of desired employee qualifications into knowledge, skills and attitudes. Adapting from Arnold, Robertson, and Cooper (1991), we construe these categories in the following way (see also Levy et al., 2001b).

- *Knowledge: Understanding and recalling of facts, information and concepts necessary for successful performance.*

- *Skills: Behaviors, including higher-order cognitive or interpersonal processes, involved in the effective execution or management of specific tasks.*

- *Attitudes: Socioemotional or affective feelings and dispositions, including level of motivation to carry out tasks, as well as orientation to coworkers and team processes.*

The new generic competencies sought by international corporations taking part in the Bikson and Law (1994) study, for example, would entail knowledge (understanding globalism in the cognitive sense), as well as skills and attitudes (for translating that understanding into successful context-specific performance). The research approach described below makes use of this typology, as well as specific frequently mentioned attributes in the reviewed literature for eliciting the characteristics of successful career professionals in internationally oriented organizations.

**DEMAND-SIDE PERSPECTIVE**

Although our literature review addressed both the potential supply of international expertise (by examining data from relevant educational institutions) and the demand for it as expressed in publications by or about likely employers (Lindstrom, Bikson, and Treverton, 2002), our primary data collection procedures focus chiefly on competency needs from the perspective of the demand side.

First, our research concerns how globalization has changed the human resource requirements of organizations with an international reach; in this way, it assumes that these organizations' increasingly global missions provide an appropriate basis for assessing the adequacy of the supply of desired competencies. Second, the research targets those who are moving toward higher-level managerial and professional positions in their organizations—those who are in the leadership pipeline. It is difficult to make inferences from educational data about programs offered or numbers graduating in them to the likely supply of internationally competent managers and professionals at mid-career and beyond. For both reasons, we concentrated our primary data collection efforts on employing organizations.

As noted earlier, the project presupposes that international leadership today is shared among government agencies, for-profit organizations, and non-profit institutions (both intergovernmental and nongovernmental).[2] Consequently, we construe the demand for international competencies as distributed over these three sectors. Within them, the study takes as its focus the managers and professionals who are expected to be successful at directing mission-based activities

---

2 Between 1978 and 1998, the number of international nongovernmental organizations increased more than sixfold (from 289 to 1,836), yet their human resource needs in general and their leadership needs in particular are disturbingly underrepresented in relevant research literature (Lindstrom, Bikson, and Treverton, 2002). There is also very little research literature on the 21st-century competency needs of intergovernmental organizations, in spite of their growing stature and significance in the conduct of international affairs.

with international implications.  While this orientation does not focus attention on human resource needs at the lower levels of organizational hierarchies, it is not restricted to the top tiers.  Rather it addresses the larger cadre of career employees that influence in significant ways the nature of critical business processes that have an international reach.  These ranks constitute the supply of candidates for top-level leadership, either in their own organization or in others.

# CHAPTER THREE.   RESEARCH APPROACH

Our research approach is based on work done in prior RAND projects, along with the main findings from the literature review as outlined above.   Primary data are gathered through structured interviews, supplemented by unstructured discussions of emerging issues with knowledgeable experts.   Below we describe the research approach in more detail.

## PARTICIPANTS

To gather primary data, the project drew a purposive sample of 75 organizations divided equally among the public, for-profit, and non-profit sectors.   Organizations had to meet two criteria for inclusion. First, they had to have international missions that engage them in interactions spanning national boundaries.   Second, they had to have been in existence long enough to have experienced the effects of increasing globalization.   We set the cutoff at five years, but most of the organizations in our sample have been in operation for far longer.

Within these fairly broad criteria we sought, in each sector, variation in mission orientations.   For instance, in the for-profit sector, we included both manufacturing and service firms, representing both traditional and high-technology industries.   In the public sector, we solicited the participation of agencies involved in defense, national security, and diplomacy, but we also sought a range of agencies typically seen as responsible for developing and implementing domestic policy.   And in the non-profit sector, we recruited foundations, humanitarian organizations, and intergovernmental institutions.   The attained sample, comprising 76 organizations in all, is listed in Appendix A.[3]

---

3 Although the project targeted an attained sample of 75 organizations, it instead gathered data from 76 (with 26 organizations included from the non-profit sector).   We

Then, within each participating organization, we attempted to identify, by role, two types of individuals to take part in structured interviews: a high-level human resources department representative and a high-level line manager for a border-spanning business process. Typically the human resources representative was selected first; that individual then suggested candidates who could fulfill the second role. Structured interviews were carried out with a total of 135 individuals, distributed as shown in Table 3.1.[4]

**Table 3.1 Research Participants by Role and Sector**

| **Role** | **Sector** | | | |
|---|---|---|---|---|
| | Public | For-profit | Non-profit | Total |
| Human resources | 19 | 21 | 26 | 66 |
| Line management | 22 | 21 | 26 | 69 |
| Total | 41 | 42 | 52 | 135 |

Finally, we also sought the participation of individuals who could provide insights on emerging issues in the research from a broader set of perspectives. For this purpose, we selected 24 individuals on the basis of nominations from the project's advisory group (see footnote 1), their established expertise in domains of interest, their contributions to relevant literature, or all of these. In this group, we included representatives of the supply side of the human resource picture, as well as representatives of intermediary organizations (e.g., recruiting,

---

began recruitment with a list of 30 or more organizations per sector, assuming that some would not be able to participate for reasons of corporate policy, lack of time or interest, and so on. After September 11, 2001, we eliminated from our slate some private sector organizations that had been directly affected by those events (e.g., two airline companies and a few financial services firms headquartered in the World Trade Center area) and added to our replacement list. In the end, one firm we had not expected to take part actually ended up participating. Thus the non-profit sector sample includes one more organization than the other two sectors. We do not believe that this difference materially affects the findings.

4 The number of respondents is less than 150 chiefly because not all of the targeted individual participants had the time or interest to be interviewed in the project's time frame. And, in the case of some organizations, an appropriate human resources representative could not be identified (either because human resource decisionmaking was decentralized and carried out below that level or because it was centralized to a higher level than the participating organization).

consulting, or research organizations) that assist employers in understanding and meeting their needs for an internationally competent cadre of senior managers and professionals. Many of them have held senior posts in more than one of the sectors of interest to this project. These participants are acknowledged in Appendix B.

**PROCEDURES**

Interviews were guided by a written protocol to ensure that comparable information relevant to the key research objectives outlined above would be collected systematically across participants. In the interviews, we explored effects of globalization and probed in some detail the need for new competencies to respond to the requirements of globalization. After identifying needed skills, interviewees were first asked about their views as to how well these needs are being met. They were then asked to comment on postemployment development and other efforts intended to yield higher-level cadres of internationally capable managers and professionals within their organizations and in society more broadly. Finally, they were asked to describe the issues, problems, and prospects of globalization facing their organizations. Incorporating both closed-ended and open-ended items, the protocol was flexible enough to elicit rich and wide-ranging responses. Requiring about an hour, on average, to complete, these interviews were conducted during the period from October 2001 through March 2002.

The resulting information was treated in two ways. Where closed-ended questions were asked, responses were coded using predefined categories or rating scales. Open-ended responses were recorded verbatim and subsequently summarized.

To complement and extend what we learned from structured interviews, at the end of the primary data collection period we carried out a series of unstructured interviews. These discussions chiefly addressed the last key research objective cited above. That is, they sought insights into the kinds of policies and strategies that could improve the development of leadership capabilities in internationally oriented organizations. They also solicited comments on themes and questions emerging from the structured interview data.

## ANALYSIS APPROACH

Study results are based on analyses of both quantitative and qualitative data. Where interview responses were appropriate for standardized coding, they are treated quantitatively both for descriptive purposes and for purposes of assessing the extent to which systematic differences arise as a function of sector or role. Either chi-squared tests or analyses of variance are employed, depending on whether the responses are categorical in nature or represent five-point scale ratings.[5]

For each set of quantitative findings, related qualitative data are then examined to help corroborate, interpret, refine, and illustrate what has been learned. The results are presented in the chapter that follows.

---

5 All analyses relied on SAS (Statistical Analysis System) software, version 8; SAS is a standard statistical package with programming and database management capabilities.

## CHAPTER FOUR.  RESULTS

Study results are organized into five major sections below, paralleling the key research objectives.  Within these sections, quantitative findings are typically presented first, followed by a discussion of qualitative data.  The last section is an exception, in that it relies exclusively on qualitative material.

We employ the following conventions in presenting quantitative findings.  First, the number of responses (n) varies somewhat among interview items as a function, for instance, of respondents' knowledge about a question or its applicability to their organizations.  Thus, in the tables below, we present frequency data as percentages for ease of comparison across items, but we also indicate the total number on which these percentages are based.  Where averages are provided, we also indicate the number of responses they reflect.

Second, data tables organize responses to interview questions by sector.[6]  Although the analyses we undertook examined all responses for variation as a function of both role and sector, role differentiation proved to be rare.  (Where it occurs, we report it.)  The determination

_____

6 For purposes of drawing a sample of international organizations and exploring what can be learned about similarities and differences in human resource needs at senior managerial and professional levels across sectors, we grouped together in the "non-profit" category both nongovernmental organizations (e.g., humanitarian institutions such as Oxfam and philanthropic foundations such as Kellogg with intergovernmental organizations such as the United Nations and affiliated institutions such as UNICEF and UNDP).  This procedure yields a very heterogeneous category.  For instance, intergovernmental organizations are restricted by member government funding and hiring guidelines, while most nongovernmental organizations are not.  Thus, in some respects intergovernmental organizations face constraints like those faced by US federal agencies, while some nongovernmental organizations are as free as for-profit firms with respect to human resource practices. We have nonetheless combined these international entities in our analyses because of some relevant similarities.  First, they comprise major alternatives to US government employment for international career candidates who want to pursue public service.  Second, their number and salience--plus their partnering roles with government agencies, for-profit firms, and one another in the conduct of international affairs--has increased dramatically in the last decade or two (Lindstrom, Bikson, and Treverton, 2002).  Readers should bear in mind the heterogeneity of the "non-profit" category when interpreting findings from the study.  Where relevant, the report calls attention to differential

of statistical significance of differences between responses grouped by
sector or role is based on a .05 confidence level at minimum, indicating
that the obtained result would have occurred by chance only five times
in a hundred (or less). The tables also typically provide values for
the statistical test used, where significant, along with the associated
probability levels.

Qualitative material is usually summarized by sector in relation
to the questions under discussion. When respondents are quoted, they
are usually identified only by sector to preserve confidentiality.

## EFFECTS OF GLOBALIZATION

Globalization, as defined above, refers to the increasing
interdependencies that develop from growing types and numbers of
interactions that span national, as well as sectoral boundaries. One
key research objective has to do with learning whether and how
globalization trends have affected organizations like those that are the
focus of this study.

The profoundly disturbing events of September 11, while
underscoring the significance of transborder interactions, at the same
time made salient the dark side of global networks. For this reason,
structured interviews first inquired about the impact of September 11;
then they asked respondents to address the overall consequences of
greater globalization for their organization in general and for its
human resource needs in particular.[7]

Below we discuss, in order, responses to these two sets of
questions.

---

responses from nongovernmental and intergovernmental participants in the study, relying
chiefly on qualitative data.

7 This research, with a focus on the implications of growing globalization in general,
was begun and interview instruments were developed and pilot tested well before September
11. The consequences of the September 11 events for organizations with international
missions could not, however, be ignored. We therefore revised initial parts of the
interview protocol to take them into account. Organizations that had already participated
in the interview before that date were recontacted for responses to the new items;

**Impact of September 11**

Structured interviews began with a question about the extent of impact of the events of September 11 on the participant's organization and then asked about the nature of those effects. Answers to the initial question are shown, by sector, in Table 4.1.

**Table 4.1 Will the Events of September 11 Have A Significant and Lasting Impact on Your Organization?**

(in percentage)

| Response categories | Sector | | |
|---|---|---|---|
| | Public | For-profit | Non-profit |
| Little/no significant impact | 15 | 35 | 15 |
| Significant but short-term impact | 39 | 17 | 27 |
| Significant and lasting impact | 46 | 48 | 58 |

Notes: $n = 133$; $x^2 = 9.4$; $p < .05$.

While a large proportion of respondents in each sector anticipated a significant and lasting impact from the events of September 11, representatives of the non-profit sector are substantially more likely than others to report such major effects; line managers and human resource officers did not differ in their estimate of the September 11 impact. Types of effects mentioned by a sizeable percentage of respondents overall include the following: security (mentioned by 58 percent of all respondents); line operations (51 percent); economic consequences (35 percent); geographic orientation (30 percent); and organizational partnerships (19 percent). When probed, 54 percent of interviewees also recognized human resource effects.

Across sectors, interviewees immediately cited intensified security concerns for employees on travel, especially for those traveling overseas. Many organizations altered their travel policies in response, and a sizeable number of interviewees pointed to increasing

---

additionally, some organizations in the targeted sample that had been directly affected by those events were replaced with others.

reliance on networked information and communication technologies as a travel substitute, where feasible. At the same time, a number of organizations voiced concerns about potential terrorist threats to their technology infrastructures. Economic effects were in the foreground as well. According to participants from the for-profit sector, the events of September 11 only worsened an already bleak economic environment. For public agencies and non-profit institutions, on the other hand, economic effects were mixed: Programs aligned with the implicated geographic regions or policy domains received increased funding, while others experienced loss of visibility and support. Organizations in the United Nations community, in particular, expressed concern that issues of terrorism could eclipse the broader global agenda. Interviewees were uncertain about how long such effects would persist.

More complex, and potentially more lasting, are reported effects on mission-based operations and associated organizational partnerships. In the for-profit sector, chief operational consequences had to do with geographic orientation: Firms doing business in Muslim countries experienced severe international relations problems both abroad and at home. In the non-profit sector, many organizations increased their efforts to assist the Afghanistan region, while others renewed their commitment to fight poverty and inequality—the perceived root causes of terrorism.

Public sector respondents, however, reported the most notable impact—the need for a fundamentally different approach to their missions, as illustrated in these comments by interviewees from different agencies.

> In times past, foreign adversaries behaved in ways that corresponded to our systems. There were clear divisions between foreign and domestic, law enforcement and defense, civil and military. Now the situation is that foreign is impacting the domestic. It's a different reality—blurring the lines.

> There is priority given in defense policy and international affairs policy . . . to not only the impact on foreign countries of the US role abroad, but also the relationship to the domestic environment. This must now be calculated in very different ways.

> The bureaucratic structure of the government is not optimal for
> dealing with crises of the kind that occurred on September 11.
> There is increased emphasis on how to reorganize to efficiently
> and effectively deal with threats.

> Sharing will actually happen now . . . . The difference is that
> there has been a real effort toward more integrated steps between
> agencies that didn't happen before.

These comments emphasize the interweaving of globalization with
domestic affairs and highlight the importance of new partnerships across
varied US federal agencies. Additionally, respondents called attention
to the need to partner with other governments to accomplish their
international missions, as well as the need for more flexible and agile
processes to replace fixed, slow bureaucratic operations. Government
agencies appear to have lagged behind for-profit and non-profit
organizations in realigning their missions with the realities of growing
globalization.

Finally, the events of September 11 were perceived as having a
number of human resource consequences. Across sectors, respondents
anticipated more difficulties hiring foreign talent in the future; this
concern was most pronounced in public sector agencies. Respondents
generally believed it would also be harder to get US employees to
relocate abroad. Further, many representatives of the for-profit sector
commented that in the aftermath of September 11 there is increased
recognition of the need to hire or train higher-level employees for
management in ambiguous and difficult situations. However, in the
public sector, these events produced one very positive outcome: A surge
of patriotism has boosted agencies' ability to recruit job candidates.
As one respondent put it, "People have a lot of confidence in the way
government is handling the crisis, and there are many who want to be a
part of it." It was unclear how long this effect would endure.[8]

---

8 Survey data reported by The Brookings Institution in a May 2002 publication titled
Opportunity Lost (Mackenzie and Labiner) show that less than a year later, public trust
and confidence in the federal government and support for its leaders--which had risen
sharply in the aftermath of September 11--had fallen back almost to the same levels as
before those events. These trends are consistent with findings released in September 2002

**Globalization Affects All Sectors**

Following the discussion of September 11, respondents were asked to comment more generally about the impact of globalization on their organization in recent years. Again the interview first inquired about overall effects and then probed for more specific human resource implications. Table 4.2 summarizes, by sector, answers to the general question about effects of recent globalization trends.

**Table 4.2 How Have Globalization Trends Affected Your Organization in Recent Years?**

(in percentage)

| Response categories | Sector | | |
|---|---|---|---|
| | Public | For-profit | Non-profit |
| Few/negligible effects | 2 | 24 | 6 |
| Some/moderate effects | 17 | 27 | 58 |
| Many/major effects | 81 | 49 | 36 |

Notes: n = 134; $x^2$ = 31.6; p < .0001.

As these data make clear, public sector interviewees are more likely than their counterparts in other sectors to report many or major recent effects, and the difference is highly significant. Qualitative data indicate, however, that this cross-sector variation is primarily a consequence of the for-profit and non-profit sectors having gotten a much earlier start on globalization. In contrast, as suggested by the previous results, federal agencies are only beginning to cope with its implications (e.g., the blurring of foreign and domestic affairs).

**Importance of Transnational Interactions Has Increased**

The definition of globalization referenced above mentions the transnational exchange of ideas, goods, services, and money. To tap this dimension of globalization, the interview asked respondents to

---

by the Pew Research Center for the People and the Press in a One Year Later report indicating that the public has grown more critical of the government again (www.people-press.org).

indicate the importance of their home organization's interactions with other people, markets, and/or organizations outside the United States. A 5-point rating scale was used for this purpose, where 5 = very important and 1 = not important. The overall mean response to this item (4.6) indicates that international interactions are, indeed, quite important to the organizations taking part in the study (as we had assumed in our selection procedures). Nonetheless, there is a significant difference between sectors on this dimension (F = 3.2, p < .05); public sector representatives give distinctly less importance to international interactions (mean rating = 4.4) than do participants from the for-profit or non-profit sectors (with overall mean ratings of 4.6 and 4.8, respectively).

## Globalization Affects Hiring and Deployment of Personnel

To get a better picture of what globalization means in terms of the moving of people across borders, we asked interviewees about whether and how often their managerial and professional employees are based, deployed, or seconded outside the United States. We also asked the converse question—whether and how often their organizations engage non-US citizens in their work. Responses to both questions are shown, by sector, in Table 4.3.

**Table 4.3 How Likely Are You to Deploy US Citizens Abroad?***
**How Likely Are You to Employ Non-US Citizens Here?****
(in percentage)

| Response categories | Sector | | | | | |
|---|---|---|---|---|---|---|
| | Public | | For-profit | | Non-profit | |
| | Citizens abroad | Foreigners hired | Citizens abroad | Foreigners hired | Citizens abroad | Foreigners hired |
| Few, rarely | 31 | 75 | 25 | 26 | 19 | 12 |
| Some, occasionally | 18 | 0 | 7 | 5 | 6 | 15 |
| Many, often | 51 | 25 | 68 | 69 | 75 | 73 |

Notes: n = 130; * $x^2$ = not significant; ** $x^2$ = 44.8; p < .0001.

With respect to sending employees to non-US destinations, a majority of respondents overall say this is a widespread and frequent occurrence, and there are no significant differences by sector in this practice. Looking at the other direction of movement, however, reveals sharp sectoral differences; not unexpectedly, federal agencies are far less likely than private sector establishments in either the for-profit or non-profit sector to employ foreign nationals. Nonetheless, public sector organizations appear to be making serious efforts to create more multicultural internal environments. Their representatives are significantly more likely to report their organization has formal workforce diversity goals (72 percent) than their counterparts in the for-profit and non-profit sectors (46 percent and 60 percent, respectively).[9] Types of workforce diversity targets most often cited, overall, include gender (mentioned by 55 percent of all respondents); race or ethnicity (51 percent); and international representation (30 percent).

Attracting and retaining US minority candidates for international careers are described as especially problematic for public sector agencies. Besides requirements to meet Equal Employment Opportunity requirements, representatives of federal government organizations cited many other reasons for pursuing a diverse workforce.

- *We strive to "represent the face of America," to "reflect the values of the public writ large."*

- *"Diversity helps productivity." "Greater creativity" and "better ideas" result "when many different perspectives are represented."*

- *Diverse workforces "help organizations blend into the diverse environments" in which they are working.*

- *Public sector agencies "have a responsibility to model good behavior."*

While they seek greater minority participation in their international career paths, however, the federal agencies taking part in

---

9 Responses to this question also differed by role; human resource officers were significantly more likely than line managers to report that diversity goals are formal

this study find themselves—as one interviewee put it—"somewhat hamstrung" for two kinds of reasons. First, there is not a lot of diversity among US citizens pursuing degrees in relevant masters or doctoral programs in this country (see also Lindstrom, Bikson, and Treverton, 2002). Second, public sector organizations believe their salary limits make them unable to compete successfully with the private sector for talented minority candidates.[10] For-profit firms, however, also report a shortage of minority candidates with interests in and qualifications for working abroad. Such candidates, they say, are in great demand among all international firms "to mirror, and thus to better serve, the customer base" in the United States as well as in the global marketplace.

In addition to striving for certain demographic characteristics in the composition of their workforce, organizations could, potentially, respond to globalization by seeking different kinds of career employees. Interviewees' responses to our questions about the kinds of employees they need are shown in Table 4.4.

**Table 4.4 With Trends Toward Globalization, Does Your Organization Now Need Different Types of Employees?**
(in percentage)

| Response categories | Sector | | |
|---|---|---|---|
| | Public | For-profit | Non-profit |
| Few/no differences | 24 | 47 | 31 |
| Moderate differences | 34 | 33 | 45 |
| Major differences | 42 | 20 | 24 |

Notes: n = 129; $x^2$ = 8.6; p < .10 (marginal significance).

ones (rather than informal). We interpret this difference to reflect human resource officers' greater familiarity with official personnel policies in their organizations.

10 A Brookings Institution report, however, finds little evidence that government can win the recruiting battle with higher pay alone. While minority candidates are more likely than others to choose public service, public service now takes place in many different settings. So, according to the Brookings survey, young people who have already made the decision to spend their careers serving the public are quite likely to head for the private sector, with non-profit organizations becoming a destination of choice (Light, 1999, 2000). The report concludes that, while pay is important as students consider first jobs, it is far less important than the nature of the job itself.

Overall, about one-third of interviewees report negligible effects of globalization on the kinds of career employees they need; the other two-thirds report moderate to major changes in human resource needs. Although the sectoral differences are only marginally significant, they suggest that public sector organizations perceive greater effects of globalization than other sectors do on their human resource needs at present; this finding is consistent with the view that the public sector has arrived late in coping with globalization.

**Changes in Technologies and Environments Drive Human Resource Needs**

Open-ended comments describe several factors perceived as driving the changes associated with globalization. The worldwide diffusion of networked information and communication media, for instance, enables an organization's headquarters to remain in close contact with far-flung field offices while permitting many kinds of business processes to operate on an "anytime, anywhere" basis. At the same time, there are a host of new domains reflecting scientific advance or social change (or both) that require advanced, specialized knowledge; these range from biotechnology and nano-engineering to environmental protection, resolution of intellectual property disputes, and micro-enterprise management. And even traditional fields require new orientations. Several interviewees, for example, noted the need for global or, at least, regional economists (rather than country economists).

At the same time, organizational structures are changing. Levels of hierarchy are being reduced and stovepipes are being dismantled in efforts to create more agile, effective business processes. For instance, United Nations headquarters and other organizations in the intergovernmental community describe moves toward decentralization, with increased decisionmaking responsibility for field officers, and toward greater lateral cooperation across "silos." Further, new cross-organizational and cross-sectoral partnerships have become part of the global landscape. As one consultant put it, today's problems are "bigger than any customer—no one agency, or even one nation, has these problems within its purview." According to another, globalization has meant that foreign policy now includes a whole host of actors: NGOs (nongovernmental organizations), foundations, universities, the private sector. It becomes a challenge to determine what the government should be doing and . . . what the comparative advantage of government will be. Also, as a third expert explained, "By now, the government needs to treat NGOs . . . as a normal part of making foreign policy." Striking a succinct summarizing note, a fourth expert said that you can "be a public leader without being in the public sector."

Finally, in the eyes of one international expert interviewed, before September 11 the costs of cross-border connectivity "had been going down, down, down—and we expected an increasingly frictionless future." This expectation was dramatically challenged, and, as a result, "how we see the world is changing." Most noteworthy, before September 11 the success of globalization had been measured chiefly in economic and financial terms. "Now we realize we must take a broader view and assess globalization in terms of geopolitical and social trends." He added that this "should and will have a long-term and significant impact on how international organizations operate." The next subsection explores the kinds of competencies organizations believe they will need to operate effectively as globalization progresses.

## COMPETENCIES FOR INTERNATIONAL CAREERS

As the preceding findings establish, participants in the three sectors of interest to this study have experienced significant organizational consequences attributable to globalization, ranging from effects on missions and operations to effects on internal structures and extramural partnerships. While government agencies have been slowest to come to terms with globalization, the events of September 11 intensified and altered its impact across all sectors. Changing human resource needs are part of the globalization picture as well. The findings that follow describe perceived human resource needs in more detail.

**Problem Solving, Strategic Thinking, "People Skills" in Demand**

In the course of the interview, respondents were provided a list of 19 attributes that surfaced frequently in the project's literature review as key ingredients for successful career performance in international organizations. They include very generic knowledge, skills, and attitudes (e.g., "substantive knowledge in a technical or professional field"), as well as qualities thought to play a special role in missions with a global reach (e.g., "cross-cultural competence") or in advancing toward leadership (e.g., "ability to think in policy and strategy terms"). Respondents were asked to assess the significance of these characteristics "for effective performance in an organization with missions like yours," using 5-point rating scales (where 5 means very important and 1 not important). Table 4.5 summarizes the resulting judgments by sector; it also provides the overall importance rank and mean rating for each attribute.[11]

---

11 For purposes of presenting summary data about all 19 rated attributes in one table, we have omitted F values in favor of indicators of statistical significance levels for each analysis of variance by sector found to be significant.

**Table 4.5 What Makes A Successful Career Professional in An
International Organization?**

| Attribute | Means for Rated Importance | | | | |
|---|---|---|---|---|---|
| | Overall Rank | Overall Mean | Public Sector | For-profit Sector | Non-profit Sector |
| General cognitive skills (e.g., problem solving, analytical ability) [t] | 1 | 4.6 | 4.7 | 4.7 | 4.5 |
| Interpersonal and relationship skills | 2 | 4.6 | 4.6 | 4.5 | 4.6 |
| Personal traits (e.g., character, self-reliance, dependability) | 4 | 4.4 | 4.5 | 4.3 | 4.4 |
| Written and oral English language skills * | 8 | 4.1 | 4.3 | 4.0 | 4.0 |
| Foreign language fluency *** | 19 | 3.2 | 2.9 | 2.9 | 3.7 |
| Substantive knowledge in a technical or professional field * | 12 | 3.9 | 3.6 | 3.9 | 4.1 |
| Knowledge of international affairs, geographic area studies *** | 14 | 3.6 | 3.9 | 3.2 | 3.8 |
| Managerial training and experience [t] | 18 | 3.4 | 3.2 | 3.3 | 3.6 |
| Cross-cultural competence (ability to work well in different cultures and with people of different origins) ** | 5 | 4.4 | 4.3 | 4.1 | 4.6 |
| Internet and information technology competency | 17 | 3.5 | 3.5 | 3.5 | 3.5 |
| Ability to work in teams | 6 | 4.3 | 4.3 | 4.3 | 4.4 |
| General educational breadth | 16 | 3.6 | 3.6 | 3.5 | 3.7 |
| Multidisciplinary orientation | 13 | 3.8 | 3.8 | 3.9 | 3.7 |
| Ambiguity tolerance, adaptivity | 3 | 4.5 | 4.5 | 4.5 | 4.4 |
| Empathy, nonjudgmental perspective ** | 11 | 4.0 | 4.0 | 3.6 | 4.2 |
| Innovative, able to take risks | 10 | 4.0 | 4.0 | 4.2 | 3.8 |
| Competitiveness, drive *** | 15 | 3.6 | 3.7 | 4.1 | 3.2 |
| Ability to think in policy and strategy terms *** | 7 | 4.2 | 4.3 | 3.9 | 4.5 |
| Minority sensitivity | 9 | 4.1 | 4.1 | 3.8 | 4.2 |

Notes: n = 135. Each attribute was rated for importance where 5 = very important, 1 = not important, and 3 = moderately important. The following annotations are used to indicate significance of differences in rated importance of attributes by sector (no annotation indicates differences are not statistically significant): *$p < .05$; **$p < .01$; ***$p < .001$; [t]$.05 < p < .10$.

Among the top-ranking characteristics, skills and attitudes predominate; less importance is accorded to knowledge, whether in particular professional/technical domains or in international affairs. Qualitative data suggest this is because specialized subject matter knowledge is moving forward rapidly, while operating environments are constantly changing and becoming more complex. So what has been learned in the past is subject to obsolescence. This is not to say that professional/technical knowledge is viewed as unimportant, but rather that it has to be continuously acquired. Being able to learn and to solve problems is in the long run more important than any present-day knowledge. If people have generic cognitive skills, according to a private sector representative, "The required technical skills can be taught." Echoing this point, a non-profit sector interviewee added that, "The true challenge is to grow people all the time."

Further, although high-ranking competencies tend to emphasize skills and attitudes over knowledge, they are more or less evenly divided among those competencies that would promote effective performance in any type of organization (e.g., "interpersonal and relationship skills") and those more aligned with effective performance when organizational missions have a global reach (e.g., "ambiguity tolerance, adaptivity"). Interviewees explained that longstanding needs for generic capabilities have not diminished—if anything, they have increased. Rather, new internationally oriented competencies have been added to their prior human resource requirements.

As Table 4.5 indicates, there is reasonable congruence across sectors about the relative value of many of the attributes rated.[12] Analysis of variance turned up significant differences between sectors for only about half of them. Notable differences include the following:

- *The for-profit sector, not surprisingly, places significantly more importance on competitiveness and drive than do the other sectors.*

- *Both the for-profit and non-profit sector respondents give a significantly higher rating to substantive knowledge in specific professional or technical areas than do public sector interviewees.*

_____
[12] Very little difference is observed in importance ratings as a function of respondent role, with the exception of two attributes. Line managers attach significantly more importance than human resource officers do to personal traits such as character, self-reliance, and dependability (p < .01). On the other hand, human resource officers attach marginally greater importance to substantive knowledge in a technical or professional field than do line managers (.05 < p < .10).

- *The non-profit sector accords significantly more importance to cross-cultural competence than the others do.*

- *The ability to think in policy and strategy terms is valued especially highly by the non-profit and public sectors, as is the ability to take an empathic, nonjudgmental perspective.*

- *Public sector respondents give significantly higher ratings to English language proficiency than do the others. In contrast, non-profit sector respondents give markedly higher ratings than others do to foreign language fluency.*

**Functional (Not Academic) Foreign Language Skills Highly Valued**

Given the international orientation of this research, we were interested to learn why foreign language fluency ranked at the bottom of the list. Qualitative data are enlightening on this point. On the one hand, fluency in a specific foreign language may reflect academic mastery of literary usage that is not necessarily functional in real-world task contexts; serious negotiations will always require professional translators. On the other hand, becoming skilled in a second or third language is treated as a proxy for the kinds of knowledge and attitudes that effective leadership in international mission domains will presuppose. The following comments from participants are illustrative.

"We are in a multicultural world; the greater language capabilities we have, the better we can relate."

"You cannot work internationally without learning languages. It is critical for cultural understanding."

"It is hard to quantify the benefits of a foreign language, but there are real dividends."

"In many respects we don't need a second language, although it is an indicator of somebody with a broader global perspective."

"We get credibility when working on projects abroad if we can speak with our local counterparts—especially with those that are nonprofessional."

The bottom line, then, is that—even though more people abroad are speaking English than ever before and even though professional translation will always be needed for conducting official international interactions—respondents overwhelmingly endorse foreign language learning as a significant contributor to the cross-cultural competency required for the successful conduct of global missions. What, then, explains the stunningly low ratings given to foreign language fluency per se? The apparent disconnect is explained by participants' views that foreign language fluency, as developed and assessed by academic institutions, is typically not by itself sufficient to produce cross-cultural competency. Most university programs emphasize literary (e.g., reading and writing) rather than applied (e.g., spoken social or business interaction) uses of foreign languages. Such programs may also be supplemented by studies abroad. Even so, according to respondents, students often live in expatriate quarters, take courses from US university professors, and socialize chiefly with one another. Thus, while gaining fluency, they may not be acquiring cross-cultural competence. This finding is highly consistent with results from previous RAND research (Bikson and Law, 1994; Berryman et al., 1979) and helps explain the importance accorded by respondents to real-world international experience in subsequent career development (see the discussion of career development, below).

### Recruiting Strategies Vary More by Sector than Skill Needs

To supplement the list of competencies for international professionals and managers derived from the literature review, we asked respondents to tell us what was missing that had proved to be important in their organizations. For-profit sector respondents tended to emphasize individual attitudes; they seek, for instance, integrity, resilience, self-confidence, initiative, and so on. Those in the non-profit and public sectors, in contrast, gave more attention to sociopolitical knowledge, skills, and attitudes. Characteristics such as "diplomatic skills," "political savvy," "networking capabilities," and "ability to work in coalitions" (across institutions) received frequent mention. Additionally, respondents in both of these sectors underscored the need for people who could "sell ideas" and be "results oriented," attributes that have long been well regarded in the for-profit sector.

In principle, then, the three sectors could all be competing for the same talent pool. In practice, however, at the entry level, the talent war is not as intense as might be expected; organizations in the three sectors appear to recruit career employees from different places. Table 4.6 provides responses, by sector, to questions about where organizations look to identify strong career candidates.[13]

### Table 4.6 Where Do You Most Often Find The Kinds of Career Candidates You Want To Recruit?
(in percentage)

| Sources | Sector | | |
|---|---|---|---|
| | Public | For-profit | Non-profit |
| Business schools | 11 | 55 | 2 |
| Academic graduate departments | 49 | 32 | 43 |
| Public policy schools | 47 | 17 | 33 |
| International programs | 58 | 17 | 29 |
| Undergraduate departments | 22 | 46 | 8 |
| Recruiting firms | 0 | 43 | 4 |

Notes: n = 127. Responses fell into three categories (often, sometimes, and rarely/never a good source). The percentages above reflect those in each sector who reported that the itemized source was "often" a good one. All sources reflect highly significant sector-based differences, with values of $x^2$ ranging from 18.7 to 48.0.

As the data in Table 4.6 show, the for-profit sector relies heavily on recruiting firms ("head hunters") together with business schools and undergraduate academic departments as sources of strong career candidates-far more so than the other two sectors. Qualitative information from respondents suggests several reasons why these practices are not more widespread. The cost of employing search firms

---

[13] In Table 4.6, we present data for one response category only (percentage of respondents indicating their organization "often" finds good career candidates through a particular source; we do this to facilitate comparisons across highly used sources by sector using a single table. (We did not show the percentage of participants reporting

is prohibitive for government agencies and non-profit institutions, and it is difficult to recruit from business schools because good candidates have salary expectations that exceed what organizations in these sectors are prepared to offer.

On the other hand, while for-profit firms often have aggressive recruiting relationships with undergraduate academic departments, respondents in the non-profit and public sectors believe that new baccalaureate-level graduates are not sufficiently seasoned—they need more experience. Consequently, the non-profit and public sectors are more likely to turn to graduate academic departments, where the for-profit sector also (but somewhat less frequently) locates good career candidates. The public and non-profit sectors also rely very heavily on graduate schools' public policy or international programs, where for-profit firms are much less likely to recruit. Besides these sources, 74 percent of interviewees mentioned other avenues for locating career candidates, most notably personal contact networks, the web, and advertising in select media (professional publications, as well as major newspapers and news periodicals).

**Candidates with Specialized Skills Needed to Fill Gaps**

How well do organizations' recruitment and selection strategies work to provide them with the competencies they seek in international career employees? Interviewees were asked to answer this question using a 5-point rating scale (where 5 = very well and 1 = not well). The overall mean response (3.7) indicates that these procedures are perceived as working, but in mediocre ways; that perception is quite uniform across sectors.[14]

---

that they only "sometimes" or else "rarely/never" find the itemized source a good one for career candidates.)

14 There are, however, significant differences in evaluation of these activities by role (F = 6.2; p < .05); human resource officers rate recruitment and selection strategies as substantially more effective (mean = 3.9) than their peers in line management (mean = 3.5).

Open-ended comments from interviewees indicate that—even though the economic downturn means there are more job candidates today than in the 1990s—some needed competencies are nonetheless in short supply. Representatives of each sector cited specialized professional or technical positions that are hard to fill (e.g., micro-enterprise analysts, international accountants, organizational development professionals, scientists, and engineers in varied domains), as well as positions that are hard to fill because of requirements for fluency in particular languages or familiarity with particular areas of the world (e.g., Japan, China, and developing countries).

For example, for-profit firms stressed the difficultly of locating individuals with the requisite knowledge, skills, experience, and willingness to be deployed abroad. In the public and non-profit sectors, positions requiring scientific and technical expertise in areas related to international missions are often hard to fill because the pay is not competitive with what could be earned in the for-profit sector. Additionally, non-profit organizations say they lack people who are able to "sell" ideas. But far more frequently, respondents across sectors emphasized the shortage of career candidates with multiple integrated competencies. Organizations with global missions need expertise in a technical or professional field plus management skills and international experience. (The combined capabilities become even more important at mid-career levels and beyond.) In today's environment, according to an interviewee from the United Nations community, most institutions would not be comfortable with a trade-off among these competencies.

As a result, across sectors, three-fourths of the participants in this study say their organizations have positions left unfilled for lack of good candidates. When asked how they cope with such shortages, the responses were remarkably similar across sectors. The most common workarounds are the following.

- *Many organizations try to "do more with less," spreading their existing staff too thin. This option is less than desirable because it may result in "slowing down operations" or "doing a bad job."*

- *Another frequent response is to keep the post open, engage in more aggressive recruitment, explore new labor markets, and wait until a viable candidate is located. In for-profit firms, such delays may mean that business opportunities are forgone. In the public and non-profit sectors, remaining out of a particular international arena may not be an option. In such cases, in-house expertise may need to be reorganized or redeployed to staff the mission, creating shortfalls elsewhere.*

- *A third approach is to relax the requirements. Most participants say this usually means opening the position to a more junior employee than was sought, with the hope that even if there are short-term problems the experience will turn out to have long-term value as an investment in human resource development.[15]*

- *A final common strategy is to rely on consultants or contractors. While widespread, this practice is regarded as having two disadvantages. First, according to interviewees, it usually turns out to be expensive (both in regular costs and in transaction costs). Second, it results in turnover and loss of institutional memory (instead of building a reusable knowledge base).*

Besides these frequently used workarounds, some organizations are able to increase the compensation package for a particular position. Others may offer a "referral bonus" to employees for locating good candidates upon their accepting the job and/or offer candidates who take such unfulfilled posts a "signing bonus." None of the coping strategies, however, are regarded as viable long-term solutions to filling mission-based human resource needs in international organizations. In the next section, we look at what such organizations do to align their workforce competencies more closely with their needs at senior managerial and professional levels.

---

[15] Although respondents to this interview indicated that job level is the only requirement they are likely to relax, the literature reviewed for this project (see Lindstrom, Bikson, and Treverton, 2002) suggests that foreign language requirements are also frequently relaxed.

**CHALLENGES OF CREATING A LEADERSHIP CADRE**

Findings presented in the previous section suggest that, apart from some highly specialized qualifications, organizations are not having difficulty finding career employees with the substantive professional or technical competencies they need. Rather, what they lack are individuals who combine such competencies with managerial skills and international vision and experience—the kinds of individuals who should comprise the future leadership cadre in organizations with a global mission.

Literature reviewed for this project (see Lindstrom, Bikson, and Treverton, 2002) views postemployment professional development as one of the main vehicles by which organizations attempt to create a better fit between the workforce capabilities they have and those they need. Lateral hiring affords another major approach to that goal. Here we explore how the organizations taking part in this study make use of such options.

**Career Development Programs for Mid- and High-Level Managers**

Table 4.7 summarizes data about postemployment development efforts in the organizations we studied.

**Table 4.7 Does Your Organization Offer Postemployment Development Opportunities at Different Career Stages?**
(in percentage)

| Response categories | Sector | | | | | |
|---|---|---|---|---|---|---|
| | Public | | For-profit | | Non-profit | |
| | Early | Mid-career | Early | Mid-career | Early | Mid-career |
| Few, none | 6 | 13 | 7 | 40 | 10 | 35 |
| Some | 23 | 17 | 33 | 17 | 43 | 51 |
| Many | 71 | 70 | 60 | 43 | 47 | 14 |

Notes: n = 126. Differences in development opportunities early in the career are not statistically significant; for mid-career and beyond, development offerings differ significantly by sector ($x^2$ = 35.4; p < .0001).

Overall, a majority of respondents report that their organization provides many opportunities for development after career employees have

been hired; while there are variations in the distribution of
opportunities across sectors, the differences are not statistically
significant. Although development activities are also provided at the
mid-career level and beyond, the frequency of such offerings decreases
markedly in the for-profit and non-profit sectors. By contrast, a
sizeable majority of public sector respondents report the frequent
offering of development programs for employees at later career stages.
And, at later career stages, the between-sector differences in
development opportunities are highly significant.

Besides inquiring about the extensiveness of career development
offerings at varied levels, interviews also asked about the types of
education or training undertaken. Table 4.8 shows the percentage of
respondents, by sector, who cited frequent use of a particular
development approach.

**Table 4.8 How Frequently Are Different Types of Postemployment Development Offered?**

(in percentage)

| Types of development | Sector | | |
|---|---|---|---|
| | Public | For-profit | Non-profit |
| Course work * | 95 | 95 | 78 |
| On-the-job training * | 75 | 93 | 78 |
| Job rotation ** | 42 | 42 | 20 |
| Internships *** | 19 | 54 | 2 |

Notes: n = 125. Responses fell into 3 categories (often, sometimes, and rarely/never offer a particular type of program). This table shows percentages, by sector, who say a particular type of program is often offered. Sector differences in use of all four development approaches are statistically significant (*p < .05; **p < .01; ***p < .001), with values of $x^2$ ranging from 10.5 to 33.0.

## Courses and On-the-Job Training Dominate Professional Development

By far, course-based instruction and on-the-job training are the
most heavily used development approaches, although there are significant
differences as a function of sector. For example, the for-profit and
non-profit sectors give about equal emphasis to formal classes and on-
the-job training; in the public sector, formal classes dominate. Job

rotation and internships are less widespread, in general, with for-profit sector interviewees reporting far more frequent use of internships than their counterparts in other sectors.

In addition, over 70 percent of respondents mentioned other developmental techniques such as mentoring, coaching, job shadowing, and cross-functional training. We then asked interviewees to estimate how much their organizations invest, as a percentage of annual payroll, in professional human resource development.[16] As shown in Table 4.9, average expenditures range from 4.7 percent (public sector) to 3.0 percent (non-profit sector), with an overall average of 3.8 percent. The differences between the sectors in human resource development investments, as estimated by respondents, are only marginally significant. However, the direction of difference is consistent with the finding (above) of more frequent development offerings throughout later career stages for public sector employees.

**Table 4.9 Estimated Annual Expenditure, as A Percentage of Total Payroll, on Professional Development**

| Means by Sector | | |
| --- | --- | --- |
| Public | For-profit | Non-profit |
| 4.7 | 4.5 | 3.0 |

Notes: n = 70. Overall mean = 3.8%; F = 2.7; p < .10 (marginal significance).

**Development Programs Ineffective for Training Global Leaders**

How well do these investments in human capital development for career employees pay off? Interviews asked respondents to judge how effective their early-stage career and late-stage career development approaches are for providing their organizations with the competencies

---

16 The question about investment in professional development was expressed in this way to allow for comparability of responses among organizations that differ in size and in pay scale. Only slightly over half the respondents were able to provide estimates on this basis, however, so the data should be regarded as suggestive rather than as reliable indicators.

they need to enact their global missions.  Responses, elicited on 5-point rating scales, are summarized in Table 4.10 (where 5 = very effective and 1 = not effective).

**Table 4.10 How Well Do Professional Development Programs Work at Different Career Stages?**

| Career stage | Means by Sector | | |
|---|---|---|---|
| | Public | For-profit | Non-profit |
| Early career | 3.6 | 3.5 | 3.6 |
| Mid-career and beyond | 3.7 | 3.7 | 3.5 |

Notes: n = 119.  Effectiveness was rated on a 5-point scale where 5 = very effective, 1 = not effective, and 3 = moderately effective. None of the differences between sectors at either career stage are statistically significant.

Despite the substantial initial and continuing investments made in career development, organizational representatives taking part in this research do not judge them to be particularly effective in providing the international experts and expertise they need.  This lackluster evaluation is similar across sectors and across roles as well—that is, human resource officers share this conclusion with their counterparts in senior line management.[17]

A review of qualitative data gathered from the three sectors indicates that the terms most frequently used to characterize later-stage career development activities are "self-initiated" and "ad hoc." While individual development plans are often filed as a part of performance review procedures or to establish that employee training objectives are being met or both,[18] these person-specific efforts are

---

[17] There are no significant role-based differences in judgments about the effectiveness of early career or later-stage career development activities; human resource officers and senior line managers alike give them equally mediocre ratings.

[18] The Government Employees Training Act (GETA), which was passed in 1958, amended in 1994, and given a boost by the Government Performance and Results Act (GPRA), helps explain why the public sector reports an abundance of development offerings for employees at mid-career levels and beyond.  However, it is not clear how extensively these options are used or how well they support organizational missions when employees take advantage of them.  Most training is arranged by individual employees and their supervisors in Individual Development Plans; typically, there is no higher-level link established between

rarely linked to the organization's strategic plans and are unlikely to cumulate to yield the competencies critical to future international leadership. Further, the most widely used approaches (e.g., courses) are those least likely to yield the learning desired (e.g., integration of substantive and managerial skills). Thus, as one for-profit sector interviewee explained, there are enough development programs being offered, but they need to be more structured and targeted. Moreover, according to respondents from the non-profit sector, there is "no culture of training" and "no passion for training" at higher career levels.

**Lateral Hiring Rarely Used to Develop Global Leadership Skills**

As a complement to career education and training for acquiring the competencies they need, international organizations may also engage in lateral hiring to remedy human resource shortfalls at upper hierarchical levels. Overall, 45 percent of interviewees report this is a frequent practice in their organizations (and most common, according to respondents, in public sector agencies).[19] The interviews also inquired, when organizations hire laterally, how often they seek higher-level career candidates from within the same sector. Responses to this question are summarized in Table 4.11.

---

these and competencies implicit in either future workforce goals or agencies' strategic plans.

19 Although lateral hiring in general appears to be fairly common across sectors, it is more frequently cited by respondents from federal agencies than by private sector respondents; however lateral hiring in the public sector is frequently from other public sector organizations--and sometimes from the same parent organization.

**Table 4.11 When You Hire Laterally, How Frequently Would It Be from The Same Sector?**

(in percentage)

| Response categories | Sector | | |
|---|---|---|---|
| | Public | For-profit | Non-profit |
| Rarely, never | 7 | 9 | 10 |
| Occasionally | 38 | 13 | 51 |
| Often | 55 | 78 | 39 |

Notes: n = 123; $x^2$ = 13.6; p < .01.

As the data in Table 4.11 indicate, patterns of lateral hiring differ markedly between sectors. For-profit organizations, for instance, tend most often to hire from within the same sector. Qualitative responses indicate that, although most firms prefer to "grow from within," there are times when they have higher-level positions open that they cannot fill internally. However, when they hire senior professionals and managers laterally, they tend to hire not only from firms in the same sector but also in a very similar business domain. That is because, according to comments from experts, it would be extremely risky to have top-level decisionmakers who are not thoroughly grounded in the industry's core business processes. Moreover, according to interviewees, the public and non-profit sectors do not nurture the skills and attitudes valued in the for-profit sector, and the environment they represent is too different from the environment for leaders in the for-profit world.

The non-profit sector exhibits more mixed patterns, with significantly greater openness to lateral hiring outside the sector than is evidenced by its counterparts in other sectors when filling higher-level vacancies. Qualitative responses show this sectoral difference is mainly attributable to foundations. Like their for-profit counterparts, humanitarian and intergovernmental organizations in the non-profit sector tend, when hiring laterally, to seek candidates from same-sector institutions engaged in highly similar lines of work. Foundation respondents, in contrast, say they seek to fill higher-level vacancies with individuals from other sectors who will bring energy and fresh perspectives. Said one foundation interviewee, "It is easy to get lax when you are in a giving position."

The public sector falls somewhere between the practices of the other two sectors; over half the respondents indicated that, when lateral hiring is involved, the senior manager or professional most often comes from another public sector agency. The existing Intergovernmental Personnel Act (IPA) makes it possible for employees to move across agencies but does not make it easy or especially desirable. The IPA could instead be transformed into a distinguished learning opportunity for international career employees, and its use for that purpose should be expanded—as should other programs that detail government officials to the Congress--to state and local governments, or to the private sector. In fact, it is easiest to fill open higher-level posts with a candidate from a parent agency (because so many of the hiring hurdles will already have been cleared). In contrast, it is difficult to fill such positions with candidates from outside the public sector because of salary differences (a problem government agencies share with humanitarian organizations) and also because of the very long time the government hiring process takes to complete. Strong senior candidates with international expertise are often lost to the private sector during the wait.[20] Further, in many agencies there is cultural resistance to welcoming outsiders who, as one interviewee described it,

---

[20] Some progress is under way toward reducing hiring delays in the public sector. For instance, some agencies have moved away from paper-based application processes to automated ones. Others have introduced systems of conditional employment, where offers are extended to promising candidates even before completion of background checks, physical and psychological examinations, and so on; and, in some agencies, these processes can be completed between the time a summer intern has gone back to the university and the time of graduation when full employment begins. In one agency, for example, such measures have reduced hiring times from roughly six - nine months to about three - six months. For higher-level positions, the Presidential Appointment Initiative, carried out by The Brookings Institution in partnership with the Pew Charitable Trusts, analyzed the conditions that render the presidential appointment process intrusive, overly complicated and time consuming. The initiative has released a number of reports with recommendations for streamlining these procedures (see www.appointee.brookings.org/about_PAI.htm).

"haven't put in their time." It is, according to another government interviewee, "a difficult paradigm to break."

**Global Leadership Skills Lacking, Biggest Gap in Public Sector**

In the end, then, the mix of lateral hiring plus professional development approaches we have described does not improve the overall assessment of how effectively the combined measures in place work to meet international competency needs at higher organizational levels. On a 5-point rating scale (where 5 = very effective and 1 = not effective), the mean response to this question is 3.5, with no significant differences as a function of sector or respondent role.

The outcome—a shortage of desired competencies in the future leadership cadre for international organizations—is reflected in Table 4.12. As these data suggest, all types of international organizations are experiencing shortages of needed competencies at higher professional and managerial levels. This is not surprising, given the continuing pressures of globalization and their intensification after September 11 (see above). However, the extent of the problem varies markedly across sectors. As evidenced in Table 4.12, for example, over two-thirds of for-profit sector respondents report that few to none of the critical competencies required for their global missions are lacking at higher organizational levels. And, although the non-profit sector reports a larger lack of needed competencies, the shortfall is by far most pronounced in the public sector—notwithstanding the greater number of mid-career development opportunities that sector provides its employees (see Table 4.7).

**Table 4.12 Are There Competencies for International Career Employees That You Find in Short Supply at Mid-Career Levels or Higher?**
(in percentage)

| Response categories | Sector | | |
|---|---|---|---|
| | Public | For-profit | Non-profit |
| Few or no competencies lacking | 29 | 71 | 32 |
| Some competencies lacking | 45 | 20 | 61 |
| Many/major competencies lacking | 26 | 9 | 7 |

Notes: $x^2$ = 22.1; $p < .001$.

Although the severity of the shortfalls may vary across sectors, qualitative data make it clear that their nature is essentially the same. According to respondents in the for-profit sector, it is difficult to find people at mid-career and higher levels with technical and managerial skills, along with international knowledge and well-developed political skills. One interviewee from the non-profit sector described the competency shortage as "T-shaped," referring to a combination of breadth of internationally oriented managerial and interpersonal skills together with substantive depth. Said another, "Currently missing is leadership with deeper knowledge of how the international system works." Putting the point differently, a United Nations interviewee underscored the need for "national US decisionmakers who can 'play' at the international level."

Many public sector respondents likewise emphasized the serious challenge of finding people with strong managerial skills in addition to professional competence and international experience. In particular, a broad perspective is missing for many at middle and senior career levels: "They understand their own job well but need a wider perspective on the mission of the agency," commented one interviewee; another observed that cultural competency is "always in short supply." As a result, some public sector participants called their organizations

"neckless" because of the lack of a senior level leadership cadre
between top-level officers and lower-level line employees.

It appears, then, that efforts to create a leadership cadre have
met with mixed success to date among the globally oriented organizations
taking part in this study. There is widespread agreement about the
qualities that are critical to international leadership in today's
world—they entail the integration of substantive depth, managerial
ability, and cross-cultural competence, along with a broad strategic
vision of the organization's mission. The data discussed above suggest
that the public sector lags the others in creating such a leadership
cadre.

## FUTURE DIRECTIONS

We began the interviews for this research with questions about the
recent past—about the effects of globalization on organizations' human
resource needs as they positioned themselves to carry out their
international missions. The interviews ended by asking participants to
look ahead—to comment on promising as well as problematic prospects for
meeting their needs for leadership as they faced the 21st century world.
The responses to both sides of this question are summarized in Table
4.13.

**Table 4.13 Looking Ahead, What Do You Foresee for Your Organization:
Future Human Resource Problems?\*  Promising Human Resource Prospects?\*\***
(in percentage)

| Response categories | Sector | | | | | |
|---|---|---|---|---|---|---|
| | Future Problems | | | Promising Prospects | | |
| | Public | For-Profit | Non-Profit | Public | For-Profit | Non-Profit |
| Minor, hardly any | 12 | 46 | 35 | 10 | 46 | 33 |
| Some, moderate | 27 | 39 | 61 | 45 | 31 | 65 |
| Many, major | 61 | 15 | 4 | 45 | 23 | 2 |

Notes: n = 129; $^*x^2 = 44.7$; $p < .0001$; $^{**}x^2 = 33.0$; $p < .001$.

Projections of the likely state of human resources in these global
organizations over the next five to ten years vary significantly by

sector, as indicated in Table 4.13. Perhaps not surprising in view of the findings discussed above, public sector respondents foresee substantially more serious human resource problems than their peers in for-profit and non-profit institutions. Paradoxically, they also envision markedly more promisingly human resource prospects than their counterparts. Qualitative data shed more light on these assessments.

**Demographics and Other Factors Portend Shortage of International Leaders**

Across sectors, demography and cohort effects are cited as factors in future human resource shortfalls. The baby boom generation is near retirement, but downsizing and hiring caps in the 1980s and early 1990s have seriously vitiated the future leadership cadre. All sectors will be affected to some degree by these trends. However, sector-specific personnel policies and hiring constraints mean that they are creating the most severe problems for the public sector. As one expert put it, government "can't afford to have more than a quarter retire, leaving only the mediocre and the young behind." And this problem is exacerbated by bureaucratic and procedural rigidities in the process of getting a good candidate hired in most federal agencies. A public sector interviewee commented that the "ossified federal government personnel system is meant to address a lot of concerns other than attracting and retaining a quality workforce." According to another expert, these trends sum to "a human capital crisis for the federal government."

A second reason why human resource shortages at senior levels are expected to worsen concerns the combination of managerial skills and deep competency in an organization's primary business processes, plus international knowledge and experience. As explained earlier, integrated substantive and managerial capabilities are already scarce in all three sectors. Further, finding individuals with these capabilities who are internationally knowledgeable and experienced, as well as willing to relocate to a post abroad is even more difficult. Again, the public sector will be hit hardest by this shortfall. As one federal agency interviewee noted, those who possess cultural sensitivity along with the requisite domain knowledge are in short supply for a job that is "physically risky, personally inconvenient, and for which there is no extra incentive to be there—like pay." This is so, said another expert, even though such "job-based experiences" are "clearly . . . a major factor in an individual's personal development as a leader."

In the for-profit and non-profit sectors, international expertise has often been acquired either by hiring consultants or by hiring foreign nationals. Consultants, however, cannot provide leadership, and foreign nationals may become even more difficult to hire in the future than they have been in the past. Public sector respondents also noted these difficulties, and the hiring hurdles already described only intensify the obstacles to hiring non-US citizens in their organizations.

A number of more specific future shortages surfaced as well. For instance, representatives of the for-profit sector mentioned the near-term—and probably long-term—shortage of senior managers and professionals with advanced skills in science, mathematics, technology, and engineering. For some lines of business, these competencies are critical to sound decisionmaking about policies and strategies. As one expert explained, that kind of background is vital "not just to manage risks but to see the wave before it breaks." While US graduate schools turn out excellent candidates in these domains, they are increasingly likely not to be US citizens and therefore to confront future hiring obstacles.

In contrast, the non-profit sector called attention to its growing need for people with a detailed understanding of economics, finance, global markets, information systems, and a host of related domains that are business school staples. A major barrier for this sector is not a supply shortage, but rather the inability of many of its constituents to pay salaries that are competitive with what master of business

administration candidates can earn in the for-profit sector. This
difficulty also confronts the public sector.

**Opportunities to Build New Leadership Are Unprecedented**

Against this background of negative expectations, what are the
promising prospects on the human resources horizon? In the near term,
the lagging economy means that organizations in a position to hire will
have a wealth of candidates from which to choose. In particular, the
dot-com downturn has enabled public and non-profit organizations to
acquire needed information technology (IT) professionals at salaries
that would not previously have been competitive. On a more positive
note, respondents say that each new cohort of employees is more IT-savvy
and more motivated to keep up with state-of-the-art IT uses.
Technological advances, in turn, can leverage the workforce in many
ways. In particular, it widens the eligible pool of employees—
telecommuting, for instance, permits hiring people who are homebound or
who live far away, including in other countries.

Another positive trend for the future state of human resources in
international organizations, according to interviewees, is a general
awakening of interest in and an increasing knowledge about international
affairs. Study participants say this trend has been in evidence for
some time and was boosted by (but not initiated by) the events of
September 11. Organizations in the United Nations community report they
foresee continuing gains in "prestige" and "reputation" as well.

Finally, both public and non-profit sector representatives say
that, at present, there is greater interest than ever in serving civic
goals in the United States and in contributing to humanitarian goals
abroad. As one non-profit sector interviewee put it, people now believe
they will "get more satisfaction with being parts of solutions to big
problems." Thus, the most serious future problem for the public sector—
a large human resource gap in the leadership cadre as the baby boom
retires—could become its best hope if it is able to devise ways of

attracting and retaining the high-caliber employees it seeks to provide leadership for its growing global missions.

Most public sector participants and many of their private non-profit sector counterparts believe, in fact, that the circumstances outlined above combine to afford an unprecedented opportunity to address their human resource shortfalls, attracting new talent and revitalizing their future leadership cadres. Interviewees from both sectors cited, as a first step in the process, doing a better job of assessing their strategic competency needs and engaging in more aggressive, targeted recruiting. Some federal agency respondents said they would also aim to "sell" the work, taking advantage of the improved perception of government service and renewed interest in globally challenging missions.

Taking this tack may have the effect of bringing public sector agencies into closer competition for talent with major non-profit sector organizations that have long relied on their ability to sell their service missions. For the effort to succeed, however, several public sector interviewees said the agencies would concurrently have to make big reductions in the hiring timeline and also to exploit more fully the tools and flexibilities at their disposal to offer more competitive pay or other incentives.[21]

**Innovative Personnel Policies and Practices Needed**

Further, attracting the right kinds of new employees is only part of the solution to the human capital problem. Another part of the solution has to do with retaining and nurturing them so that they will, in the end, make effective contributions to international leadership in the organization. Toward this goal, public and non-profit sector

---

[21] It should be acknowledged that use of special authorities for hiring and paying outsiders is not entirely unproblematic. As noted above, some senior career employees regard it as unfair that outside executives with little government experience are coming in at higher pay levels. Further, these flexibilities are also underused, in part, because there is no money backing them up.

representatives said they would have to do a much more careful job of professional development at mid-career levels and beyond. According to some, they also need to devise flexible arrangements for enabling valued employees to move in and out of their organizations, developing viable career portfolios. The lifelong career model is not applicable to the world of work today, so all sectors need to learn how to support and to gain benefit from mobile careers.

Implementing such changes, in turn, will demand considerable innovation on the part of human resource departments. Here the public sector faces another barrier, in part because of the longevity of senior employees in their personnel departments who have internalized government civil service rules and have not been encouraged to act entrepreneurially on behalf of their organizations. Referring to his own experience with personnel and human resource managers, one federal agency representative said, "It is difficult to find someone to think strategically and to be innovative, someone with a base of knowledge, experience, and energy." Across all sectors, interviewees agreed that human resource departments would have to become more like strategic partners with highest-level decisionmakers if their organizations are to become better positioned to exercise international leadership in the 21st century.

## POLICIES AND PRACTICES RECOMMENDED BY RESPONDENTS

The preceding discussion of findings calls attention to many sectoral differences in effects of globalization, desired workforce competencies, and ways of acquiring them. However, the nature of the anticipated human resource shortfalls for meeting international leadership challenges in the coming years is remarkably similar across the sectors.

Organizations with global missions will increasingly need individuals who integrate substantive depth and managerial strength with international vision and cross-cultural competence. Presently the need is most acute at mid-career and higher levels because the baby boom generation is nearing retirement while the downsizing strategies of the late 1980s and early 1990s severely reduced the successor cohorts. Recommended approaches for addressing these problems are largely applicable across sectors as well. Ease of implementing changes in human resource policies and practices may well differ by sector, especially given regulations and rigidities that constrain the behavior of public sector organizations. Nonetheless, the commonalities seem to outweigh the differences.

Thus in what follows, we group the observations of our interviewees by the types of policies and practices they recommended, rather than by sector. These recommendations are drawn chiefly from qualitative material gathered in unstructured discussions with diverse experts and are supplemented with information elicited in structured interviews. For convenience, their recommendations are presented in order of likely ease of implementation.

## Use Technology to Leverage the Current and Future Workforce

Many of the organizations participating in this study reported an increased use of networked information and communication technology, including videoteleconferencing capabilities, as a substitute for travel in the aftermath of September 11. These experiences should provide a foundation for exploiting networked media more effectively to leverage an internationalized workforce.

First, according to study participants, these technologies could be used more extensively to reduce distances among field offices and between them and headquarters, making it easier to stay in contact with colleagues worldwide. Having a supportive information and communication infrastructure in place for US employees overseas should alleviate some of the risks associated with mobility today, while helping to overcome the feeling of disconnectedness from the home organizations that often accompanies extended expatriate assignments. It might thereby alleviate problems associated with repatriation as well.

Equally important, such connectivity can be a major vehicle for promoting internationalized awareness among employees at home or abroad. Underscoring its value for this purpose, one expert noted that his corporation had introduced a global Internet package that makes it very easy to stay "connected with clients and worldwide teammates." Since the mid-1990s, the organization has had a daily global forum to which its distributed employees regularly contribute, along with weekly global teleconferences. Similarly, an interviewee from the non-profit sector emphasized the value of these kinds of exchanges for soundly integrating global thinking with local thinking.

Finally, several participants recommend exploring the use of digital media to hire individuals abroad with specialized scarce competencies and to allow them to work from the home country. Across sectors, there was a concern that hiring non-US citizens for jobs in the United States may be more difficult in the future (for instance, if fewer visas are issued). On the other hand, networked information and communication technologies might permit international organizations to locate and engage as telecommuters people with specifically sought foreign language fluencies. One international organization already emails documents for translation to field offices where the language is not uncommon; translations are then returned by email (overnight, if the need is urgent).

Other specialized competencies where foreign nationals are often sought are those required in some fields of science, technology, engineering, and research and development. But people with such competencies typically have to coordinate their work closely with others on project or process teams. Thus, according to another private sector participant, taking advantage of networked media to enable the effective use of distributed international teams would also demand expertise in managing virtual organizations. As a cautionary note, however, representatives from all three sectors pointed out that increased reliance on information and communication technologies would have to be accompanied by commensurate increases in system security safeguards.

## Collaborate More Closely with the Supply Side

As a first step toward getting good international career employees into the pipeline, respondents noted the importance of maintaining continuous relationships with sources of good candidates (schools and professional societies). During periods of cutbacks, many organizations neglected these relationships. In hindsight, they recognize the importance of keeping up recruiting relationships even when there is little hiring under way.

According to one government agency representative, it is "vital to remain a reliable and conscientious opportunity for talented young people." Others concurred, pointing out that having a steady stream of candidates cuts the time needed to rebuild relationships with varied sources when there is a need to hire. At the same time, it is critical to recruit more aggressively, by "selling the work." Said another public sector interviewee, we can "go toe to toe with any corporation because of the work . . . , We have great branding." While image creation and branding are not new recruiting tools in the private sector, experts agreed, they could be used to much greater advantage now by public and non-profit sector institutions.

Employing organizations are also urged to collaborate more closely with academia to ensure that desired competencies are articulated and developed. This is important, according to one for-profit sector interviewee, because "corporations usually identify forecasted needs before academia does." (See also the following subsection.) Besides articulating specific competencies, experts underscored the need to stress to academia the value of "on-the-ground" experience as preparation for careers in international organizations. Said one, "The best and smartest kids will fail unless they have some experience abroad." Another commented that even organizations with only small international exposure want people who are "sensitive to and cognizant of cultural differences." They therefore look for "hard experience—time on the ground elsewhere." However, this recommendation will not necessarily be well received by universities, according to the experts we talked with, because they chiefly promote formal coursework that advances students within an academic discipline; the value-added contribution from real-world experience is much harder to assess academically.

Consequently, international organizations should work with universities to develop programs that "promote more adventurous scholarship" and engender "a broader concept of professional achievement." Cooperative programs, internships, and other opportunities for promising students to engage in tasks that exercise and shape the desired competencies will do much to improve the supply side, especially if they involve work abroad; at the same time, they will help collaborating organizations by providing an avenue for "proactive recruiting" of high-caliber candidates. For example, one government agency taking part in this study has instituted a cooperative program in which it pays for one class per semester, and students work alternate semesters and summers at the agency during their sophomore, junior, and senior years; when they graduate, about 80 percent of students accept employment offers there. The Presidential Management Internship program also receives consistently high marks for the candidates it produces, but they are insufficient in number to address the expected future leadership shortfall in federal agencies.

While such programs enable the sponsoring organization to cull top choices from the candidate pool, other approaches aim to shape the competencies candidates pursue. Organizations with highly specific needs—for instance, knowledge in a substantive domain combined with fluency in a particular foreign language—might opt for very targeted programs subsidizing graduate education in exchange for commitment.

That is, they could support the education and professional development of individuals pursuing such competency combinations in exchange for an agreement to work for the sponsoring organization for some number of years after graduation. Or, as another expert suggested, organizations could begin by identifying candidates with strong international experience (e.g., returned Peace Corps volunteers) and then provide technical or professional fellowships to them for pursuing the sought-after substantive skills.

Branding, proactive recruiting, and work-study programs are not new, but they have not been widely implemented in the public and non-profit sectors. Nor are they not universally implemented in the for-profit sector, even among large multinational corporations. Getting such programs under way, while beneficial to universities as well as to employing organizations, will require coping with time-consuming logistic and administrative matters; thus they do not yield solutions to short-term human resource needs. In the meantime, universities should be encouraged to enlist more diverse student cohorts. In part, such efforts would help all future employees gain multicultural experience. At the same time, it will help international organizations across the three sectors meet their workforce diversity goals.

**Assess and Target Strategic Competencies**

Previous sections of this report have discussed the kinds of competencies international organizations seek in professionals and managers at early and late career stages, with a focus on building the cadre of future leaders. As several experts pointed out to us, today's decisionmakers are likely to promote senior managers and professionals who most resemble themselves—whether or not they are best suited to exercise leadership in tomorrow's world. One discussant made the point quite succinctly: "Most organizations don't know what they have or what they need in the way of competencies." Responses to the challenge of developing the cohort of future leaders should be guided by an objective approach to targeting and assessing competencies.

According to the experts we consulted, organizations should be advised to start with the development of a competency model based on their future strategic directions. The model must identify core competencies critical for success at different hierarchical levels in different key lines of business, given how the organization's international missions are planned to change or grow over time. The model should then drive objective assessments of current skill gaps, as well as future skill needs. These, in turn, can provide a more solid foundation both for targeted recruiting and for professional development of career employees already on board.

Objective competency assessment, while not unprecedented, is not widely implemented (as the heavy reliance on interviews for judging employment candidates in our sample of organizations suggests). Even where it is used, competency assessment is rarely linked to strategic directions, workforce planning, targeted recruiting, or professional development. For example, many organizations use annual performance reviews as the occasion to examine an employee's current skill repertoire in relation to requirements for promotion, and the exercise may also be used to guide future choices among professional development offerings. Most often those choices, at present, are not based on results of objective assessment methods and strategic plans. Where they are, they have proved valuable.

One government agency taking part in this study, for instance, has implemented an assessment tool for identifying gaps in managerial and professional competencies; it measures thinking skills, decisionmaking skills, leadership, teaming ability, and so on. Over the past four years, the organization has found it to be a reliable predictor of performance and uses it to guide promotions of higher-level (but not lower-level) staff. Several non-profit institutions also mentioned using competency-based methods for gauging the qualifications of prospective employees.

More systematic deployment of these methods could serve the strategic performance goals of organizations in a number of ways. First, it could link individual professional development to organizational and unit-level objectives. At present, as explained earlier, career development at mid-career levels and beyond is generally ad hoc and self-initiated. But, as one expert explained, "self-managed careers" do not cumulate to yield a corporate human capital strategy.

Second, guided by a strategic plan, competency assessment techniques could be used advantageously up and down the organizational hierarchy to inform not only hiring and promotion but to promote a culture of professional development. "Middle managers today," said one discussant, "have big tasks." Because decisionmaking has been pushed to lower hierarchical levels, these people have to understand management strategically; that is, they need to understand what is going on at levels above them (e.g., to align their unit-level business processes with broader company goals) and also below them (e.g., to manage the supply chain efficiently). As another expert urged, organizations need "leaders at every level." That is the best way to create a high-performance organization, while assuring that future top-level leadership cadres will be well supplied.

Finally, getting the right people in line for top-level positions requires giving careful thought to succession planning as well. Succession planning, our participants acknowledged, has been a buzz word for some time—but organizations should give it renewed attention, now that so many of their senior people are at the point of retiring. One expert noted that, having "pretty much dropped career management" in favor of self-initiated development, organizations "are in big trouble." Strategic competency assessment may be a vital complement to back room discussions in effective succession planning.

## Reconceptualize Career Development for International Leadership

The policies and practices discussed above would necessitate small to large incremental changes in the way organizations with global missions go about fulfilling their human resource needs. Here we summarize more innovative recommendations for developing future international leadership cadres. They present greater implementation obstacles but may afford the most promising outcomes.

Today a considerable amount of leadership development is provided through seminars, courses, workshops, retreats, and the like. While they have some potential for stimulating performance improvements, these "little self-contained training modules won't work to create global leadership," according to one expert we consulted. The limitations of such activities stem in part from their wholly generic nature: They do not provide a basis for integrating leadership with substantive competency in the organization's critical business processes, and they do not serve to link leadership to organization-specific attributes or tailor it to the culture of the organization, as well as the local contexts in which it operates. Many participants believe this helps explain why the plethora of training options do not go far toward fulfilling the need for effective international leaders in global organizations.[22]

Among more innovative approaches recommended by participants, the most commonly mentioned was the strategic use of "stretch assignments" to provide what one expert termed "career-forming" experiences. Presently, as noted earlier, stretch assignments may be used as ways of coping with competency shortfalls at senior levels; for example, an organization may send a junior-level employee with less experience than would typically be required to fill a vacant position. One respondent

---

[22] While participants in this study held generally skeptical views about the effectiveness of most leadership training courses, our literature review did not surface any systematic empirical assessments of their quality or their impact on performance.

described this practice as "taking a short-term hit for a long-term investment," meaning that there is hope that taking the risk with a junior person will pay off in career development terms. Instead of treating these as workarounds, the development experts we talked with recommend the systematic creation of such opportunities for growth.

According to this view, organizations should identify needed competencies based on their strategic plans and then create stretch assignments with coaching or mentoring that will allow mid-career people to develop into the sorts of leaders they will need. "Organizations should take risks with their people—give good junior people broader assignments that will enable growth," one expert commented.

Job rotation and cross-functional training may be used as vehicles for providing stretch assignments. However, according to the experts we consulted, development of international competence is most effectively accomplished through working on real tasks in an environment outside the home country. One of the firms participating in this study, for instance, requires completion of two such assignments, one in a developed country other than the United States and one in an "emerging" country, en route to executive leadership. Similarly, some of the non-profit institutions we studied are introducing more-systematic use of what a respondent called "to and fro" posting—a policy of rotating people between field and headquarters or across different field posts. And one federal agency taking part in the study reported it would like to create a "foreign officer corps" similar to what the State Department has for its Foreign Service Officers. Otherwise, it expects to face continuing difficulty in getting qualified career employees to go overseas.

Organizations should also explore secondments as avenues to international leadership development. "These are starting to happen, slowly," said one of the experts we talked with, adding that at present they are offered more often within organizations than between them. As an example, she cited one international corporation that has instituted a "job swap," where employees negotiate with each other and with their local managers to arrive at an agreement about exchanging positions. Sabbatic leaves also might afford an opportunity to enable employees to get "stretch" experiences. Although a university is typically the destination for employees on such leaves, sabbaticals could also serve as occasions for secondment to another organization where a desired international competency can be attained or exercised.

Finally, as the findings discussed earlier make clear, lateral hiring is another major means by which international organizations acquire the leadership they seek. And, because high-achieving employees no longer aim to spend their entire working life in a single organization, their own developmental goals have to do with building strong career portfolios. So a key question for organizations with global missions is how to make more effective use of mobility across organizations, and even across sectors, in developing future leadership cadres.

Two non-profit foundations taking part in this research have adopted time-limited contracts as a way of creating more opportunities for lateral hiring. Specifically, employees are contracted for three years' work in a position, with an option to renew once or twice; at the end of that period, they must seek other jobs (but they may look within the same organization). A representative of one of these organizations explained that "If [institution name] is to be at the cutting edge, people should not work there for a lifetime."

Less formal measures were recommended by other participants. One expert we consulted, for instance, said organizations could give much better guidance about career strategies: "They could give maps—what kinds of choices will add up to a strong career portfolio." Pointing out that even if an organization has a good program of professional career development, the outside entrant will not have been exposed to it, another expert urged organizations to give more attention to development that integrates experience with lateral transitions into the organizations. Concurring, a supply-side participant said that universities should prepare students aspiring to leadership in international careers to "move, work, and think across sectors." And, noting that government agencies often lose employees to the for-profit sector after three to five years, a public sector consultant suggested that federal agencies should also explore ways of encouraging and making it easier for such individuals to return at later career stages.

At more senior career levels, in contrast, it has typically been difficult to stimulate lateral transitions out of the public sector, both because of retirement benefit policies and policies that constrain postgovernment activity. Several experts who had made a transition from high-level federal positions to private sector posts recommend that these restrictions be reconsidered. "To permit and even encourage the cross-fertilization of leadership" these laws should be revised, said one participant; anticorruption rules and rules that prevent profiting financially from past government service "are worth having, but the current regulations are far broader than that."[23]

However, a participating expert with a strong international and cross-sector background sounded a cautionary note. In response to a query about whether in the future it will be desirable to have more moves across sectors, he said, "Yes—it exposes people to different best practices and points of view." The problem is that, "All sectors want it but don't facilitate it. They are consumers of cross-sector moves,

_____

23 The Civil Service Retirement System (CSRS), which was enacted before Social Security came into existence, is a solely defined and not portable benefit plan. In 1987, the Federal Employees Retirement System (FERS) was introduced to replace the old system, offering both Social Security and other (once vested) portable retirement benefits. About 38 percent of the civil service workforce is under CSRS. To encourage mobility, one strategy has been to allow these people to move to FERS during "open enrollment" periods. Because CSRS is widely perceived as being a more generous plan, this option did not attract much response. However, a RAND analysis (Asch and Warner, 1999) indicates that in fact FERS is more generous because expected lifetime wealth is predicted to be greater under that plan. A second constraint on mobility has to do with restrictions on activities senior public sector employees can pursue if they leave government service (see 18 USC 207). The rules are intended to prevent conflicts of interest as individuals move

not producers."  How to enable and support the development of future
leaders whose career portfolios integrate experiences across sectors, as
well as across borders, is a question that merits in-depth exploration
and policy attention.

---

into other positions and sectors that may require dealings with the government.
Restrictions are especially stringent in the first postservice year.

## CHAPTER FIVE.   CONCLUSIONS AND RECOMMENDATIONS

Increasing globalization has created an environment that makes the exercise of international leadership significantly more complex.  High-level officers of public, for-profit, and non-profit organizations must interact with one another across borders to arrive at negotiated decisions about issues that often blend advances in science and technology with policy concerns, while blurring the distinctions between foreign and domestic affairs.  Moreover, globalization is not just concerned with economics and finance; it has significant political, legal, and sociocultural dimensions—both positive and negative—that have become increasingly salient to international organizations since September 11.  The public sector got off to a slower start in coping with the broad and complex implications of globalization than the other two sectors, but, since September 11, it has been moving quickly to catch up.

### AN INTEGRATED SKILL REPERTOIRE IS NEEDED, BUT OFTEN LACKING

To exercise leadership effectively in this environment, what is needed is a multidimensional and well-integrated set of competencies. There are some between-sector differences in the extent to which particular competencies (e.g., substantive domain knowledge, competitiveness and drive, foreign language fluency versus English language communication skills) are valued, but our interviewees agree that international leaders must have an integrated repertoire of skills including:

- *Substantive depth (professional or technical knowledge) related to the organization's primary business processes.*

  Without this depth, leaders cannot make sound decisions about risks and opportunities and will not gain the respect and trust of those below them.

- *Managerial ability, with an emphasis on teamwork and interpersonal skills.*

This ability is needed not only to work with different partners but also because, within organizations, a great deal of decisionmaking is being pushed to lower hierarchical levels, making upper-level decisions more collaborative.

- *Strategic international understanding.*

It is critical for leaders to have a strategic vision of where the organization is going and to place it in a global context, while understanding the implications of operating in different localities.

- *Cross-cultural experience.*

Multicultural sensitivity cannot readily be gained through academic instruction alone. Efforts to learn a second or third language provide evidence of interest in other cultures and can form a basis for understanding them, but they are not a substitute for real world experience.

This skill repertoire is seen as being in great demand but in short supply, with the result that our interviewees expect major skill deficits in the international leadership cadre in the near future. These gaps will persist if there are not significant changes in America's approach to international career development across its sectors. Today's senior managers and professionals are nearing retirement, and it is not at all clear that succeeding cohorts have the required competencies for leadership in this changed world. While the problem has demographic and cohort dimensions that cross sectors, it is most acute in federal agencies; in reference to the public sector workforce, some have called it a "human capital crisis."

**Career Development Programs for Mid- and High-Level Managers Are Needed**

The shortage of employees with the desired repertoire of skills is greatest at mid-career levels and beyond. Regarding entry-level employees, interviewees from the organizations participating in our study are, with some exceptions, fairly well satisfied with the products of US universities. (The exceptions include a dearth of science and technology graduates, of graduates with fluency in uncommon languages, of US minorities majoring in graduate studies relevant to international careers, and of graduates with international experience.)  Typically, there is little need or opportunity for entry-level employees to exert leadership skills in an international environment, but these young people are seen as having the potential to do so.

At lower hierarchical levels, there are, moreover, alternatives to recruiting individuals with the requisite skills or developing these skills in postemployment training programs.  These alternatives include contracting out (e.g., in the case of language services); hiring non-US citizens (e.g., in the case of scientists and engineers); and establishing internships and cooperative programs (e.g., for providing desired integrative experiences in real performance settings).  There are drawbacks both to outsourcing (e.g., loss of institutional memory) and to hiring of foreign nationals (e.g., visas may become harder to get in the future), but, for now, both are viable and widely used approaches for coping with some competency shortages.  Networked information and communication technologies may also be deployed more effectively in the future to access hard-to-get skills.

Postemployment education and development programs could, in principle, address the competency shortfall among mid- and upper-level managers described above, but such programs are generally systematically designed and widely offered only at the point of entry for new employees, where the gaps between needed and available competencies are smallest.  For more senior employees, professional education and development offerings become markedly less well defined and—in the for-profit and non-profit sectors—less frequently available as well.  More important, the offerings typically provided are not well suited to yield the desired results.

Most often, career development at higher levels is self-initiated, ad hoc, and unrelated to an organization's strategic plans.  It may involve activities undertaken in order to check off a requirement or to move up a rung on a career ladder at the next performance review; or it may be a reward bestowed on those who have already demonstrated advanced leadership capabilities.  Further, the most frequently used development approaches (e.g., courses) are the least robust, while stronger programs (e.g., job rotation, especially to a non-US site) are employed much less often.  Present patterns of investment in human resource development are thus not likely to produce the needed repertoire of skills within the leadership cadre of international organizations.  Mid-career development in international organizations, then, merits targeting and strengthening.  The value-added from such investments should be directly visible in improved performance at senior levels.

## Lateral Hiring Processes Must Be Strengthened

Lateral hiring from within or outside the sector is the second potential route for remedying competency shortfalls at mid-career and higher levels in international organizations.  But for several reasons it, too, is unlikely at present to produce the mix of leadership competencies these organizations seek.  First, the stovepipe problem is replicated across organizations—that is, lateral entrants are very likely to be drawn not only from the same sector but also from very similar, narrowly defined subdomains.  Such an approach assures substantive expertise and avoids the culture shock of cross-sector transitions, but it decreases the chances of innovation and growth both for the organization and the mid-career employee.  On the other hand, cross-sector moves, while holding developmental promise for organizations and their later-career hires, are riskier, and such moves lack institutional support structures.  Finally, the public sector is at a special disadvantage for cross-sector lateral hiring at upper levels because its salary scale is not competitive and because its rules constrain the exit of its own upper-level people to other sectors.

We have identified several measures that might be taken to strengthen lateral hiring processes.  They include short-term employment contracts to encourage movement to new organizations, thereby creating opportunities for more people to gain international experience;

expansion of programs to promote cross-organization transfers in the federal government; and changes in retirement and postemployment regulations. These and other strategies could be used to provide opportunities that would be revitalizing to both individuals and organizations.

## Looking Ahead: Problems and Prospects

The end result is that the outlook for future leadership in internationally oriented organizations is very mixed—there are envisioned problems as well as promising prospects, as the discussion of study findings explained. The bad news is that, at present, these organizations lack the multidimensional competencies in their human resources that future leadership cadres will need to carry out their global missions effectively. The good news is that contemporary demographic and cohort factors combine to create an unprecedented opportunity for organizations with a global reach to repopulate their upper ranks. Further, participants in this research believe that career candidates are generally more interested in and knowledgeable about international affairs than prior cohorts; additionally they are willing to embrace mobile careers, and a larger proportion now report wanting to contribute to large-scale societal goals. Thus the public sector stands to be affected most severely by the problems that lie ahead but also stands to benefit greatly from the most promising prospects.

## RECOMMENDATIONS

What, then, can be done to take advantage of the opportunities created by the shifting demographics of the workforce and the skills and interests of these new workers to produce competent international leadership in US organizations? We recommend that US organizations that have an international reach or that are involved in preparing individuals for careers that involve an international component take the following actions:

- Encourage the development of portfolio careers.
- Develop personnel practices to support portfolio careers.
- Internationalize university curricula.

These three general recommendations, each of which is discussed below, are based on the responses of our interviewees to questions about what they would recommend to mitigate the problems and to capitalize on the favorable prospects that we have identified. Their more detailed observations are presented in Table 5.1, which summarizes both near-term and long-term solutions to the difficulties of recruiting and training international leaders in government, as well as in nongovernmental and for-profit organizations.

## Encourage Portfolio Careers

We recommend providing a mix of innovative, robust development approaches for those in mid-career and higher positions and introducing measures to facilitate the kinds of transitions between such posts that, in the end, make for the kinds of career portfolios that all sectors desire for their leaders.

Enabling the pursuit of portfolio careers will require changing mind-sets in all three sectors. The for-profit sector still prefers to grow talent within, while non-profit and public sector officials live their careers in narrow stovepipes. Within the government, the first step is to make it easier for people to move across agencies. In some areas, such as intelligence, it might be possible to mimic the experience of the military Joint Staff, making rotations to other agencies or "joint" appointments a requirement. The existing Intergovernmental Personnel Act makes it possible for people to move across agencies but does not make it easy. The provisions of this act should be expanded, and it should become a distinguished learning opportunity, as should other programs that detail government officials to the Congress, to state and local governments, or to the private sector.

The existing government career structure makes it very difficult to bring in younger mid-career outsiders, perhaps for limited terms, because doing so looks like "smuggling" them into the career system. The IPA or other ways should be found to permit such time-limited lateral moves. Bringing in senior officials from outside is easier, and it does broaden the government's leadership cadres, but it does little to develop future leaders.

The for-profit sector should begin to think of the other sectors as partners in developing future leaders. Like government, it draws on the other sectors, particularly government diplomats and military officers, for internationally oriented leaders at the top. It does not, however, think of moving its younger executives into other sectors as a way to broaden their experience.

The not-for-profit sector could play a special role in developing portfolio careers. Foundations like Ford and MacArthur have developed innovative programs from giving young people dual expertise, in area studies as well as strategy, or policy as well as science. Such opportunities could be expanded, with the specific goal of producing future leaders in all sectors with international experience and exposure. Further, as underscored earlier, international organizations within the United Nations community are playing increasingly salient and significant roles in the conduct of international affairs. It is imperative to better understand and develop US international career candidates for leadership roles in these organizations. Secondments to such intergovernmental institutions would also provide valuable stretch assignments for senior managers and professionals in US government agencies.

**Develop Personnel Practices to Support Portfolio Careers**

To support portfolio careers, the policies and strategies of human resource units and the internationally oriented organizations they serve would have to change. First, human resource units will have to become strategic partners with top-level decisionmakers charged with shaping the organization's future missions. In that capacity, they should look more broadly—even across sectors—for best practices to adopt, adapt, and implement for developing multidimensional competency repertoires in their in-house career professionals and for facilitating cross-sector lateral transitions at mid-career levels and beyond. Further, human resource units should collaborate more closely with line managers in deciding to take more risks with employee assignments (e.g., stretch assignments, especially those that involve overseas work).

Moreover, human resource units should better exploit the flexibilities that exist in current regulations and policies, while formulating new policies better designed to meet today's needs for international expertise at higher levels of organizations. The public sector faces greater challenges in this area because it has special obstacles to overcome (e.g., time-consuming hiring processes, constraints on hiring non-US citizens, and noncompetitive salaries).

## Internationalize University Curricula

Finally, to improve the supply side, the nation's education institutions need to rethink curricula and practices as they seek to produce more internationally minded leaders. They have found it easier to internationalize their faculties than their curricula, and many non-Americans now teach at America's universities. Most of those, however, have Ph.D.s from the same US universities as their American counterparts. So, these non-American faculty members with US Ph.D.s are the beginning of internationalizing, not the end.

The traditional ways that universities conceived of internationalizing their curricula—by developing academic area studies and language training—may no longer be the best ways of producing broad-gauged professionals. Instead, universities need to devise ways to give students a grounding in thinking and acting across cultures. In particular, they should ask why so many college students arrive saying that they intend to take a year of study abroad but so few actually do so.  Experiences abroad shorter than a year or semester, and more oriented toward professional tasks, might be valuable, and, given the explosion of non-Americans and of cultural diversity on many US campuses, innovative approaches could produce cross-cultural competence while students remain at home.

It is striking that internationally oriented organizations in all three sectors stress the need for a new cadre of leaders, and leadership programs are widely available in academic institutions.  Yet leadership remains something of an outcast in American higher education.  It is not quite academic, hence not quite respectable.  Yet if leaders, like entrepreneurs (or scholars) are partly born, leadership skills can also be developed.  Producing effective leadership deserves a much more prominent place in the nation's research and teaching.

**Implement Near- and Long-Term Leadership Development Programs**

The agenda for better positioning tomorrow's America to lead in a globalized world requires actions by all three sectors represented in this study, plus higher education—ideally in partnership.  Table 5.1 summarizes the chief recommendations from the study, by sector, according to whether they could feasibly be pursued to affect expected near-term international leadership gaps (first column) or would take longer and more complex implementation efforts but would address identified needs to build future cohorts of international managers and professionals.  Both courses should be pursued concurrently.

**Table 5.1 Recommended Agenda for Building International Leadership**

| | Time Horizon | |
|---|---|---|
| | **Shorter Term--The Current Workforce** | **Longer Term--The Pipeline** |
| **Public** | • Increase and enhance use of IPAs<br>• Facilitate lateral movement inside and outside government<br>• Improve hiring processes<br>• Target robust career development programs | • Expand internship and cooperative programs<br>• Narrowly target fellowships in areas of need<br>• Support and encourage portfolio careers<br>• Relax barriers to in-and-out careers (e.g., conflict of interest laws)<br>• Fund leadership development research<br>• Reserve some proportion of senior positions in any agency for the career service |
| **For-profit** | • Support career exchanges with public and non-profit sectors<br>• Target robust career development programs | • Support and encourage portfolio careers<br>• Support internationalized MBA programs |
| **Non-profit** | • Support career exchanges with public and for-profit sectors<br>• Heighten awareness of need for future leaders<br>• Improve hiring processes<br>• Target robust career development programs | • Increase funding for producing dual (and treble) expertise<br>• Increase support for leadership study and training<br>• Articulate and support study of specialized human resource needs of international non-profit organizations (both nongovernmental and intergovernmental) |
| **Higher Education** | • Promote and recognize real world study abroad<br>• Expand initiatives for internationalizing education at home | • Internationalize graduate programs in relevant areas (e.g., MPA, MPP, MBA, IP, and related doctoral studies)<br>• Rethink ways to internationalize other curricula<br>• Improve US minority recruitment/retention in international programs<br>• Give leadership development a serious place in teaching and research |

Notes: MPA – Master in public administration
MPP – Master in public policy
MBA – Master in business administration
IP – International policy

In the end, it will not be easy to respond to the challenges of 21st century leadership. In part, that is because of the complexity of the global environment that today's international organizations face. Another major difficulty is that effective responses to these challenges must be distributed over myriad organizations and will have to be largely self-generated--no one-size-fits-all solutions are in sight.

Organizations—and nations—that address these leadership challenges successfully will have a competitive advantage in the decades to come.

## APPENDIX A.   PARTICIPATING ORGANIZATIONS

**Federal Agencies**

Central Intelligence Agency
Coast Guard, International Affairs Organization
Department of Agriculture, Foreign Agriculture Service
Department of Defense, Defense Intelligence Agency
Department of Defense, Office of the Secretary
Department of Energy, Office of International Affairs
Department of Health and Human Services, Centers for Disease Control and Prevention
Department of Justice, Federal Bureau of Investigation
Department of Justice, Immigration and Naturalization Service
Department of Labor, Bureau of International Affairs
Department of State
Department of State, Foreign Service Institute
Department of Transportation, Office of the Secretary
Department of Treasury, Office of International Affairs
Environmental Protection Agency
General Accounting Office, International Affairs and Trade Division
National Intelligence Council
National Institutes of Health, Fogarty International Center
Office of Management and Budget
Office of Science and Technology Policy
Overseas Private Investment Corporation
Peace Corps
Trade and Development Agency
US Agency for International Development
XYZ Agency

**For-Profit Organizations**

Accenture
American International Group, Inc.
Bank America Corporation
Baxter International
BP Amoco
Capital Group
Cisco
Deloitte and Touche
Dow Jones
General Mills
Halliburton

Hewlett-Packard
KPMG
Merck & Company
Microsoft
Oracle
Palm Pilot
Pfizer
Proctor & Gamble
Prudential
Schlumberger
Sun Microsystems
TRW
Unocal
WorldCom

## Non-profit Organizations

American Red Cross
Amnesty International USA
Asian Development Bank
CARE USA
Carnegie Corporation
The Carter Center
Ford Foundation
Greenpeace USA
Hewlett Foundation
Inter-American Development Bank
International Monetary Fund
International Rescue Committee
International Telecommunication Union
Kellogg Foundation
MacArthur Foundation
National Democratic Institute
Organisation for Economic Co-operation and Development
Organization of American States
Oxfam America
Packard Foundation
Save the Children, United States
United Nations Children's Fund
United Nations Development Programme
United Nations Headquarters
World Bank
World Vision United States

## APPENDIX B.  EXPERT PARTICIPANTS

Ken Bertock, *Partner, McCormack & Farrow*

Walter Broadnax, *Dean, American University School of Public Policy*

Greyson Bryan, *International Lawyer, O'Melveny and Meyers*

Alison Carter, *Principal Research Fellow, Institute for Employment Studies*

Ruby Butler DeMesme, *Director, Human Capital Solutions and Defense Practices, PriceWaterhouse Coopers*

Richard Drobnick, *Assistant Provost for International Affairs, USC*

Jeanne Fites, *Deputy Undersecretary of Defense, Program Integration*

Robert Gallucci, *Dean, Georgetown School of Foreign Service*

Allen E. Goodman, *President, Institute for International Education*

Jerry McArthur Hultin, *Dean, School of Technology Management, Stevens Institute of Technology*

Robert Kimmitt, *Executive Vice President, Global & Strategic Policy, AOL Time Warner*

Ellen Laipson, *President, Stimson Center*

Alesandra Lanto, *Senior Consultant, Personnel Decisions International*

Paul Laudicina, *AT Kearney, Global Policy Business Council*

Kris Morris, *Principal, Morris & Berger*

Joseph S. Nye, Jr., *Dean, Kennedy School of Government, Harvard University*

Leonard Pfeiffer IV, *CEO, Leonard Pfeiffer & Company*

Thomas Pickering, *Vice President for International Affairs, Boeing*

Steve Roach, *Chief Economist, Morgan Stanley*

Enid Schoettle, *Special Advisor, National Intelligence Council*

Susan Schwab, *Dean, University of Maryland School of Public Policy*

Brent Scowcroft, *President, Scowcroft Associates*

Tina Sung, *President and CEO, American Society for Training & Development*

Michael van Dusen, *Deputy Director, Woodrow Wilson Center for Scholars, Smithsonian Institution*

## SELECTED BIBLIOGRAPHY

Abramson, M. A., Toward a 21st Century Public Service, Arlington, Va: The PricewaterhouseCoopers Endowment for the Business of Government.

American Council on Education, Educating for Global Competence. America's Passport to the Future, Washington, D.C.: American Council on Education.

Arnold, J., I. T. Robertson, and C. L. Cooper, *Work Psychology*, London: Pitman Publishing, 1991.

Asch, B. J., and J. T. Warner, *Separation and Retirement Incentives in the Federal Civil Service: A Comparison of the Federal Employees Retirement System and the Civil Service Retirement System*, Santa Monica, Calif.: RAND, MR-986-OSD, 1999.

Bailes, A. B., "Who Says It Can't Be Done? Recruiting the Next Generation of Public Servants," in *The Business of Government*, Arlington, Va: PricewaterhouseCoopers, Spring 2002, pp. 51-55.

Berryman, S. E., P. F. Langer, J. Pincus, and R. Solomon, *Foreign Language and International Studies Specialists: The Marketplace and National Policy*, Santa Monica, Calif.: RAND, R-2501-NEH, 1979.

Bikson, T. K., and S. A. Law, Global Preparedness and Human Resources: College and Corporate Perspectives, Santa Monica, Calif.: RAND, MR-326-CPC/IET, 1994.

Bikson, T. K., L. Cremonini, and C. van't Hof, Best eEurope Practices: Work & Skills, Leiden, NL: RAND Europe, Information Societies Technologies Programme (IST-2000-26224), 2002.

Bikson, T. K., and S. A. Law, "Toward the Borderless Career: Corporate Hiring in the 90s," *International Educator*, Vol. IV, No. 2, 1995, pp. 12-15, 32-33. Also available as RAND RP-443.

Bikson, T. K., "Organizational Trends and Electronic Media," American Archivist, Vol. 57, No. 1, 1994, pp. 48-68. Also available as RAND RP-307.

Brown, L. D., S. Khagram, M. Moore, and P. Frumkin, Globalization, NGOs and Multi-Sectoral Relations, Cambridge, Mass.: The Hauser Center for Non-profit Organizations, 37, 2000.

Finegold, D. "The New Learning Partnership: Sharing Responsibility for Building Competence," in S. A. Mohrman, J. R. Galbraith, E. E. Lawler III and Associates, eds., *Tomorrow's Organization: Crafting Winning Capabilities in a Dynamic World,* San Francisco, Calif.: Jossey Bass, 1998, pp. 231-263.

Gardner, N. W., R. B. Desmesme, and M. A. Abramson, "The Human Capital Challenge," in The Business of Government, Arlington, Va: PricewaterhouseCoopers, Spring 2002, pp. 27-30.

Gates, S. M., C. H. Augustine, R. Benjamin, T. K. Bikson, T. Kaganoff, D. G. Levy, J. S. Moini, and R. W. Zimmer, *Ensuring Quality and Productivity in Higher Education: An Analysis of Assessment Practices,* ASHE-ERIC/Higher Education Report, San Francisco, Calif.: Jossey-Bass, 2002.

Hendry, C., *Human Resource Strategies for International Growth,* London: Routledge, 1994.

Lawler, E. E., III, High-Involvement Management: Participative Strategies for Improving Organizational Performance, San Francisco, Calif: Jossey-Bass, 1986.

Levy, D. G., R. Benjamin, T. K. Bikson, E. Derghazarian, J. A. Dewar, S. M. Gates, T. Kaganoff, J. S. Moini, T. S. Szayna, L. Zakaras, and R. W. Zimmer, *Strategic and Performance Planning for the Office of the Chancellor for Education and Professional Development in the Department of Defense,* Santa Monica, Calif.: RAND, MR-1234-OSD, 2001a.

Levy, D. G., H. J. Thie, A. A. Robbert, S. Naftel, C. Cannon, R. Ehrenberg, and M. Gershwin, *Characterizing the Future Defense Workforce,* RAND, MR-1304-OSD, 2001b.

Light, P., *The New Public Service,* Washington, D.C.: The Brookings Institution Press, 1999.

Light, P., "The Empty Government Talent Pool: The New Public Service Arrives," *Brookings Review, Vol.* 18, No. 1, 20-23, 2000.

Lindstrom, G., T. K. Bikson, and G. F. Treverton, "Developing America's Leaders for a Globalized Environment: Lessons from Literature Across Public and Private Sectors." Santa Monica, Calif.: RAND, 2002.

Lobel, S., "Global Leadership Competencies: Managing to a Different Drumbeat," *Human Resource Management,* Vol. 29, Spring 1990, pp. 39-47.

Malone, T. W., and K. Crowston, "The Interdisciplinary Study of Coordination," in G. M. Olson, T. W. Malone, J. B. Smith, eds., *Coordination Theory and Collaboration Technology,* Malwah, NJ: Lawrence Erlbaum Associates, 2001, pp. 7-50.

McDonnell, L., C. Stasz, and R. Madison, <u>Federal Support for Training Foreign Language and Area Specialists: The Education and Careers of FLAS Fellowship Recipients</u>, Santa Monica, Calif.: RAND, R-3070-ED, 1983.

Morrison, A., "Developing a Global Leadership Model," *Human Resource Management,* Vol. 39, Summer/Fall 2000, pp. 117-131.

Nye, J. S., <u>The Paradox of American Power: Why the World's Only Superpower Can't Go It Alone</u>, New York: Oxford University Press, 2002.

Nye, J., and R. Keohane, "Power and Interdependence Revisited," *International Organization,* Vol. 41, pp. 723-753, 1987.

Rainey, H. G., "Competing for Talent: Special Hiring Authorities for Federal Agencies," in *The Business of Government*, Arlington, Va: PricewaterhouseCoopers, Spring 2002, pp. 56-58.

Stasz, C., "Assessing Skills for Work: Two Perspectives," *Oxford Economic Papers,* Vol. 53, No. 3, 2001, pp. 385-405.

Stasz, C., "Do Employers Need the Skills They Want? Evidence from Technical Work," *Journal of Education and Work,* Vol. 10, No. 3, 1997, pp. 205-223. Also available as RAND RP-683.

Stasz, C., J. Chiesa, and W. Schwabe, *Education and the New Economy: A Policy Planning Exercise*, Santa Monica, Calif.: RAND, MR-946-NCRVE/UCB, 1998.

Treverton, G. F. "Intelligence Crisis: What's To Be Done," *Government Executive*, Vol. 33, No. 14, pp. 18-25, November 2001.

Treverton, G. F. *Making American Foreign Policy* (casebook), Englewood Cliffs, NJ: Prentice-Hall, 1993.

Treverton, G. F. *Reshaping National Intelligence for an Age of Information*, Cambridge University Press, 2001.

Treverton, G. F., M. van Heuven, and A. Manning. *Towards the 21st Century: Trends in Post-Cold War International Security*, MR-1038.0, Santa Monica, Calif.: RAND, 1999. "Driving Forces of International Security," in Kurt R. Spillman and Andreas Wenger, eds., *Towards the 21st Century: Trends in Post-Cold War International Security Policy*, Bern, Switzerland: Lang, pp.107-164, 1999.

Ulrich, D. W., and H. Greenfield, "The Transformation of Training and Development to Development and Learning," *American Journal of Management and Development,* Vol. 1, No. 2, 1995, pp. 11-22.

Walker, D., <u>Human Capital: Meeting the Governmentwide High-Risk Challenge</u>, Washington, D.C.: General Accounting Office, GAO-01-257T, 2001.

Waterman, R. H., Jr., J. A. Waterman, and B. A. Collard, "Toward a Career-Resilient Workforce," *Harvard Business Review,* No. 72, 1994, pp. 87-95.

Wittenberg-Cox, A., "Delivering Global Leaders," *International Management, Vol.* 46, February, 1991, pp. 52-55.